Book Testimonials

"Practical, insightful and a page turning read. Tom makes short work of the much-hyped topic of artificial intelligence, drawing on decades of experience to find the pattern between a series of case studies. This no nonsense book is a must read primer for those working in the healthcare system seeking to understand the impact of AI for the sector, or those entrepreneurial thinkers looking for the business opportunities this revolution will create."

—Dr. Simon Kos
CEO, Next Practices and former Chief Medical Officer, Microsoft

Tom Lawry's new book, *AI in Health – A Leader's Guide to Winning in the New Age of Intelligent Health Systems*, will be landing on real and virtual bookshelves in hospitals and health systems at a most opportune time. After a long incubation period and much hand-wringing about potential downsides of AI, the field is now ready for prime time in healthcare. Leaders in every aspect of the industry will find practical guidance in this concise and well-written book. That includes a clear and comprehensive breakdown of the many different technologies that comprise AI as well as a discussion of the myriad opportunities to leverage AI to improve not only clinical outcomes but workflows and processes in the many support functions that make a health-care system work. The book will definitely help them cut through the morass of incomplete and sometimes conflicting information on AI and position themselves to lead the Intelligent Health Systems of the future…systems that will be powered by AI. I highly recommend this book.

—Dr. Patricia Salber
CEO, The Doctor Weighs In

"There is perhaps nothing more profound than the impact AI will have on how healthcare is delivered in the future. In his new book, *AI in Health – A Leader's Guide to Winning in the New Age of Intelligent Health Systems*, Tom shares wisdom that comes from a lifetime of experience as a business leader and technologist in the health industry. He has traveled the globe gathering insights from some of the world's most gifted experts. He examines how AI is being used in healthcare today, as well as where this powerful tech will take us in the future. There are both challenges and opportunities for AI in healthcare and Tom carefully examines both sides of the equation."

—Dr. Bill Crounse
CIO, CMIO, Senior Director, Worldwide Heath,
Microsoft Corporation (retired).

"Mr Lawry's book is a sensitively written analysis of the opportunities to use AI in healthcare whilst avoiding the pitfalls and the hype. He takes the reader through the key concepts and applies them to healthcare as only an expert in the three fields of health, technology and analytics can. Many people will be familiar with the background to the AI in health story and will struggle to know where to start and end their work. If you want to get the benefits of AI, then this book is for you. It will tell you what good looks like and how to navigate ethics, build a workforce, create new operating models and apply disruptive thinking. I loved it."

—Paul Henderson
Regional Director EMIS Health, (UK)

IN HEALTH

A Leader's Guide
to Winning in the New Age of
Intelligent Health Systems

IN HEALTH

A LEADER'S GUIDE
TO WINNING IN THE NEW AGE OF
INTELLIGENT HEALTH SYSTEMS

TOM LAWRY

CRC Press
Taylor & Francis Group
Boca Raton   London   New York

CRC Press is an imprint of the
Taylor & Francis Group, an **informa** business

A PRODUCTIVITY PRESS BOOK

CRC Press
Taylor & Francis Group
6000 Broken Sound Parkway NW, Suite 300
Boca Raton, FL 33487-2742

© 2020 by Tom Lawry
CRC Press is an imprint of Taylor & Francis Group, an Informa business

No claim to original U.S. Government works

Printed on acid-free paper

International Standard Book Number-13: 978-0-367-33684-4 (Hardback)
International Standard Book Number-13: 978-0-367-33371-3 (Paperback)

Library of Congress Cataloging-in-Publication Data

Names: Lawry, Tom, author.
Title: Artificial intelligence in healthcare: a leader's guide to winning in the new age of intelligent health systems / Tom Lawry.
Description: Boca Raton: Taylor & Francis, 2020. | Includes bibliographical references and index.
Identifiers: LCCN 2019049404 (print) | LCCN 2019049405 (ebook) | ISBN 9780367333713 (paperback; alk. paper) | ISBN 9780367336844 (hardback; alk. paper) | ISBN 9780429321214 (ebook)
Subjects: MESH: Artificial Intelligence | Delivery of Health Care—organization & administration Classification: LCC RA971.6 (print) | LCC RA971.6 (ebook) | NLM W 26.55.A7 | DDC 362.10285—dc23
LC record available at https://lccn.loc.gov/2019049404
LC ebook record available at https://lccn.loc.gov/2019049405

Visit the Taylor & Francis Web site at
http://www.taylorandfrancis.com

and the CRC Press Web site at
http://www.crcpress.com

To those who believe that health and medicine is
a noble cause and strive to make it so.

Contents

Preface and Acknowledgements

Give me a place to stand, a lever long enough and I can move
the Earth.

—Archimedes

Ours has been called the information age. There is probably no place where this rings truer than healthcare. In the 1950s, a newly minted physician would go their entire career before seeing medical information and knowledge double. Those graduating today can expect this to happen in a year or less.

Such is the challenge and opportunity for those in health and medicine today. Artificial Intelligence (AI) gives us the ability to harness the power of healthcare's data tsunami to make us better at virtually everything we strive to be better at. In this regard, AI will augment much of what we do but will not replace us... Everything about AI in health starts with humans using it to do good.

Like most of you reading this book, I've spent my entire career in and around healthcare. Whether you're running a rural clinic in the United States or you're a researcher at one of the top centers in Stockholm or London, what binds us together is this: We believe that healthcare is a noble cause worthy of our time and energy, that we can make a difference, and that there are many things about the system that challenge us to do better.

Enter the new possibilities of AI. In the hands of competent and caring clinicians, health executives, and others, our charge is straightforward—to use it to make a bigger difference than we are making today.

As the national director for AI for Health and Life Sciences at Microsoft (and as the former director of Worldwide Health), I've given keynotes and talks on AI around the world including some heady places like the Nobel

Forum. I've had the privilege of working with clinical and health leaders who are pioneering new ways of using data to push back the boundaries of health and medicine.

When it comes to my knowledge of AI, I'm reminded of what an early mentor taught me—*"none of us is as smart as all of us."* Whatever wisdom and knowledge I possess comes as part of an emerging "knowledge collective" on what AI is and how we apply it to keep people healthy and care for them when they are not.

With this in mind, there are countless people I could list as contributors to this book. Some of the most notable that come to mind include the following:

Kris Mednansky, Senior Editor at CRC Press/Taylor & Francis Group. While my name is listed as the author, Kris is really the one responsible for this book. It's a result of a chance meeting we had as I was racing to catch a flight. Her interest and persistence for a book specifically focused on AI for health leaders was the impetus for what you are reading now. She provided great guidance along the way.

John Doyle, Director Cloud and AI, Microsoft. John is one of the smartest people I know when it comes to real-world knowledge about the cloud and how clinical and business leaders can harness its power. His impatience with old-style data management is a driving force helping others transform systems and processes with cloud-based data and AI solutions. While many talk of their aspirations for the cloud and AI, John has a knack for making things real.

Harry Pappas, Founder and CEO of the Intelligent Health Association (IHA). When it comes to what intelligent health is (or is becoming), Harry's knowledge is broad and his enthusiasm infectious. Under his leadership, IHA demonstrates the power of people coming together around new or emerging technologies to share ideas and collaborate on how we understand and apply new and emerging technologies to improve the quality and effectiveness of health and medical services globally.

Ankur Teredesai, Ph.D., Professor of Computer Science and Executive Director of the Center for Data Science at the University of Washington, Co-founder and CTO of KenSci. Ankur has a unique perspective on the application of AI in health as he splits his time between academia and working with health organizations around the world in the use of AI to solve significant problems. His guidance was especially useful in ensuring that my attempts to explain AI and its uses in health in lay terms did not reduce the integrity of the information provided.

Steve Mutkoski, Worldwide Policy Director, Microsoft. Steve has a penchant for looking deeply at emerging legal and regulatory issues surrounding the use of AI in health and medicine. He sits on various national committees that create policy principles to guide policymakers and legislators. We need more people like Steve to have "eyes on" how we use AI in ways that are ethical and equitable.

Dr. Simon Kos, CEO of Next Practice and former Chief Medical Officer for Microsoft. Simon's clear-eyed "voice of the physician" combined with his global perspective was invaluable in having the content of the book fit with the clinician's point of view.

Dr. Fatima Paruk, Chief Medical Information Officer, Microsoft. Fatima's global training plus her focus and experience in population and public health helped "stress-test" some of the materials in the book.

Paul Henderson, Regional Director, EMIS Health. From the early use of machine learning and social determinants to get ahead of social issues that lead to hospitalization to spotting patterns in the outbreak of infectious diseases, Paul has done some amazing work with artificial intelligence in the United Kingdom. His feedback helped "level-set" the content found in the pages of this book to ensure it has relevance outside the United States.

I especially want to thank Jana Kralick. She has been my single best coach, editor, and critic. Without her guidance, this book would have been a giant serving of word soup. I suspect she's doing a word count and rewriting this sentence as she reads it.

And finally, a shout-out to the hundreds of talented clinicians, executives, managers, informaticists, and data scientists that I'm blessed to work with. Your creativity and dedication to the cause by using data and AI to improve outcomes and effectiveness is a constant reminder of what makes health systems around the world great.

AI is no longer about the future. It's about the present and what clinical and business leaders do now to understand and prepare for this next big shift in healthcare's computing platform.

As with most technology shifts, progress will come in fits and starts. Fifteen years ago, the capabilities of the smartphone in your pocket or purse today were unimaginable. Such is likely the case with where AI-driven healthcare is taking us. As the journey unfolds, a byproduct of AI becoming mainstream is that health and medical services will become more scientific and more human-centric in delivering better quality health services for all.

Author

After spending more than 20 years in healthcare, Tom Lawry believes that merely making the current system more efficient is akin to building a super-highway by paving over old cow paths. As National Director for Artificial Intelligence in Health and Life Sciences, and as former Director of Worldwide Health, at Microsoft, he works with innovative clinicians and health leaders who are leveraging the world's data and ever-expanding computational powers to rethink approaches to improving outcomes, quality, and satisfaction. He's a passionate advocate for harnessing the power of Artificial Intelligence to empower knowledge workers and drive meaningful reform of health systems around the world.

Tom lives in Seattle. When not working, he can be found hiking the trails of the Pacific Northwest, traveling the world to find his next favorite place or exploring the beaches near his home on the Oregon Coast.

Chapter 1

The Future Is Not
What It Used to Be

Every Generation Needs a Revolution.

—Thomas Jefferson

The revolution has begun. Artificial Intelligence (AI) is pervasive in our daily lives and about to disrupt the world of health and medicine in ways not thought possible even a few years ago. In a world of "intelligent everything," there will be no room for unintelligent health.

What if we could detect heart disease in a single heartbeat? How about unlimited, AI-assisted virtual health consults for one dollar a visit? Sound like more AI hype? It's not. Transformative health services are happening now.[1,2] They're driven by restless individuals and organizations unwilling to accept the status quo in health.

Such change could not come at a better time. Clinical and health leaders today are faced with an unrelenting set of challenges – Ever-expanding medical capabilities. Constrained resources and staff shortages. An increasingly diverse mix of patients and consumers whose needs only grow. Merely getting better with the tools we have is not going to deliver the results we need.

A different model is emerging with AI that will eclipse current systems in delivering on the promises we make every day – To improve health while delivering greater value. To provide highly personalized experiences to health consumers. To restore clinicians to be the caregivers they want to be rather than the data entry clerks we're turning them into by forcing them to use systems and processes conceived decades ago.

Forget about the stereotype of an impersonal, robot-controlled future. Intelligent Health Systems are here. They are gaining early competitive advantages by leveraging AI and the cloud. Forward-thinking health leaders are creating new organizations and reinventing old ones to improve consumer, patient, and clinician experiences. They are doing this across all touchpoints and delivery channels.

To glimpse the future of healthcare one only needs to look to other industries further along in their AI journey. After years of promises and disappointment, AI is driving pervasive value in other sectors of the global economy. Hedge funds are using AI to beat the stock market. Companies like American Express are using AI bots to improve customer service and reduce costs. Organizations are leveraging AI as a force for social good. Microsoft's AI for Earth program, for example, is using it to fight climate change and protect endangered species.

Within the health industry, AI is a change agent being applied to a growing set of clinical, economic, and human challenges embodied in the Quadruple Aim – Improving the patient experience (quality and satisfaction). Improving the health of populations. Reducing per capita costs, all the while improving the work-life of clinicians and staff (Figure 1.1).

Real-world benefits and competitive advantages are being seen by early adopters. And the *velocity of AI's value* is increasing as computer power grows, AI solutions mature, and costs drop, thanks to the benefits of secure cloud services. These trends are beginning to permeate healthcare.

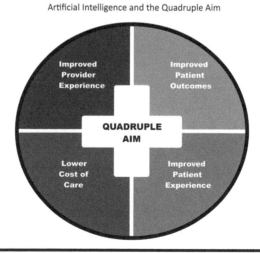

Figure 1.1   The value proposition of AI in Health directly supports the goals of the Quadruple Aim.

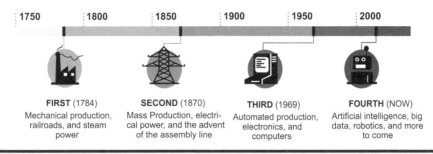

| 1750 | 1800 | 1850 | 1900 | 1950 | 2000 |

FIRST (1784)
Mechanical production, railroads, and steam power

SECOND (1870)
Mass Production, electrical power, and the advent of the assembly line

THIRD (1969)
Automated production, electronics, and computers

FOURTH (NOW)
Artificial intelligence, big data, robotics, and more to come

Figure 1.2   The four industrial revolutions. (Adapted from A. Murray, CEOs: The Revolution Is Coming, Fortune.)

They're creating almost unlimited opportunities to innovate health and medicine – For those who choose to use them wisely.

In his groundbreaking 2012 book *The Creative Destruction of Medicine*, Eric Topol, MD, brought to light in healthcare the concept of creative destruction, an economic theory first put forward in the 1940s by Austrian economist Joseph Schumpeter. Essentially "creative destruction" describes a continuous economic cycle where the introduction of radical innovation into the traditional systems becomes the real force for sustained long-term growth. As the theory goes, such growth *only comes by destroying the value of established systems and enterprises.*

The idea is that the net benefit of radical innovation, in spite of the destruction of the value of previously successful systems, is greater than if the radical innovation had never been introduced.[3]

From a historical perspective, creative destruction in action can be seen in the four industrial revolutions we've already seen. With AI and the cloud, we are in the early stages of the fourth industrial revolution (Figure 1.2).

I'm All for Change – You Go First

Change brought about by technological innovation has long triggered a diverse but predictable set of reactions. Some people are awed by the possibilities and push to be "fast-firsts." Others fear and resist the disruptive nature of the change it brings. Most are simply unaware of, or dismiss, what is happening until it affects them personally or professionally.

Whether a clinical or business leader, if you are interested in moving your career or organization towards intelligent health your challenge is twofold. First, understand your own views and commitment to the change that is occurring. Do you seek to be a "fast-first," a "fast follower" or are you hoping that AI will somehow pass healthcare by? Second, recognize and act on the fact that within any health organization there will be dedicated and talented staff whose views and reactions to such change will run the gamut of what is described above.

When it comes to leading your organization towards becoming an Intelligent Health System the greatest challenge is not the adoption of AI technology. Instead the challenge in moving your organization to the next phase is changing how people think, train, and work. Transformation using AI is not about redefining your organization's value proposition. Ultimately, it's about redesigning the organization to ensure that your mission and value proposition remain relevant in the face of new market dynamics. And while the implementation of AI throughout a health enterprise is complex, the goal for doing so is simple – To help *humans* do a better job of keeping people healthy and caring for them when they are not.

First Steps in an Ongoing Journey

In my role at Microsoft I've worked with clinical and business leaders around the world who are planning and deploying enterprise-wide AI initiatives. In the early stages of such work, I'm often struck by how many leaders are possessed with "AI envy" syndrome. This is a condition where the leaders of an organization believe that other organizations are significantly ahead of their efforts.

For anyone committed to becoming an Intelligent Health System, it's important to recognize that every health organization is early in its AI journey. A survey of traditional health systems in the United States, for example, notes that less than half have started their journey in the use of AI (Figure 1.3).[4]

Such news may be comforting for those choosing to take a "go slow" approach. But it's risky to assume others aren't moving fast.

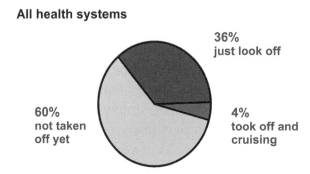

All health systems

36%
just look off

60%
not taken
off yet

4%
took off and
cruising

Figure 1.3   **Where are you on the AI/ML journey. (2019 Citius Tech "AI in Healthcare" Readiness Survey.)**

A key market dynamic that traditional providers of health services must recognize is that the competitive landscape is changing. Ever-expanding AI capabilities and the rise of the intelligent consumer are bringing a new breed of entrants into the health market. They're born as "digital-first" organizations and are focused on demolishing historical market boundaries. They move quickly. They're leveraging AI and adopting disruptive strategies with the goal of delivering better consumer experiences at lower costs. More on this in the next chapter.

Today, the move towards AI is starting to take hold within traditional health organizations. When it comes to how AI will drive value, most health systems see clinical performance improvements as the top reason for investments with improving operational performance as the next priority.[5]

Early adopters of AI in health are already seeing benefits. These include increases in informed decision making (46%), cost savings (42%), automating processes (41%), and revenue generation (41%).[6]

A study by Frost and Sullivan reports that AI has the potential to improve healthcare outcomes by 30%–40% and reduce the cost of treatment by as much as 50% in the next 7–10 years.[7] Top areas according to this global survey expected to drive the highest value for providers, payers, and consumers include:

Predictive insight and risk analysis: An emerging set of solutions are already focused on helping providers and payers assess and manage risk across the clinical, financial, and operational continuum. Early returns include measurable improvements in key metrics such as clinical quality and revenue growth.

Managing the health of populations: As value-based care takes hold across all care settings, AI will be used by organizations to predict population health outcomes and formulate smart personalized health plans. The goal here is to improve outcomes while creating a strong market differentiator.

Clinical decision support (CDS): AI-driven CDS systems will provide a framework for precision medicine. It will increase the value of existing insights, while combing and leveraging other data sets including unstructured, genomics, social, and environmental determinants.

Medical imaging and diagnostics: Powered by what are known as "deep learning algorithms," embedding intelligence into medical images is a fast-growing field designed to help clinicians find and interpret hidden disease patterns at greater speed and scale.

Drug discovery: Given the increasing burden of lifestyle-driven chronic diseases, a combination of patient-generated data with academic evidence will be critical for the future of personalized treatment options.

Patient and consumer engagement: AI-enabled digital patient engagement platforms, capable of empowering patients and providers in managing lifestyle and behavioral-based health risks, demonstrate the white space opportunity to promote preventive care practices for chronic disease management.

Three Things Leaders Should Know

With the examples noted above, seeing and believing in the power of AI in health is easy, while making it real and delivering measurable value at scale is not.

Regardless of whether you are a clinician, IT pro, or business leader, your journey towards making AI real and harnessing its power to do good starts with understanding three things that are critical to your success.

AI is different than any other tech trend you've seen or managed.

Anyone that has been in healthcare for a while knows that, when it comes to technology, we often fall prey to what's known as the "shiny object syndrome." This is where we fall in love with the idea that a new technology will, on its own, revolutionize the industry.

With this comes unrealistically high expectations. To spot which tech trend is the latest shiny object, one only needs to walk through the exhibit halls at conferences like the Healthcare Information and Management Systems Society (HIMSS) conference. Here you will see what "technology of the moment" is the shiny object. It's easy to spot as most every vendor selling their wares has it plastered across their banners and incorporated into their sales pitches.

AI has been in the shiny object category lately. So why should we act on the belief that it is somehow different?

The first thing to recognize about AI is that it creates a true paradigm shift in how data and IT systems add value. Up until now, information technology has mainly served as static data repositories that tell us something about the past and possibly the present.

Historically we've created value with these systems by dipping our "data ladle" into many pools of information. Once we "retrieve" data we then use our human capacities to evaluate the data and make decisions on everything from diagnoses and treatment decisions to a range of decisions affecting operational and financial performance.

AI upends this model. As technology that mimics human functions like vision, speech, and cognition comes into play, it is moving us to a future state where machines act more like humans. It also means that humans act less like machines in performing lower value, repetitive tasks. This blurring of the lines between humans and computers to perform tasks and predict things serves as the basis for dramatic transformation. As this happens, it requires leaders to understand and address a variety of issues relating to clinical and operational automation, staffing, data governance, and a new wave of regulatory and ethical issues.

The power of this shift allows us to rethink and automate many processes and activities. When done right, the use of AI removes the shackles of repetitive activities to empower knowledge workers to perform at their highest value. It also creates new opportunities to serve health consumers in ways that are more personalized and efficient. It is this single dynamic that sets AI apart from other technology breakthroughs and requires leaders to reexamine all aspects of how services are provided.

As you will learn in the next chapter, another critical factor driving AI and intelligent health forward is what's happening in the rest of the world. The rise of intelligent consumers and their expectations is a reality. The question is not whether intelligent systems are becoming the norm, but rather how the health industry will adapt and keep up with the revolution that is already occurring.

Consumers and businesses expect intelligent systems to make their lives better. According to data from Accenture, consumers and patients are already six times more likely to view AI as having a positive impact in the delivery of health services. This makes AI a competitive differentiator when it comes to acquiring patients and building loyalty.[8]

Once you understand how AI fundamentally shifts what machines can do, a host of new challenges becomes apparent in its application and its impact on how everyone thinks and works.

Healthcare's "data tsunami" is the new currency for intelligent health.

In the emerging world of Intelligent Health Systems data is the new currency by which health organizations will rise and fall. How you curate and manage your data estate will be as strategically important as how you manage your financial and operational assets. More on this in Chapter 12.

In many ways the march towards more data fueling the AI movement in health is nothing new. It started when medicine came out of the shadows of quackery and into the realm of being a repeatable, scientific discipline.

Take medical imaging for example. Roentgen's discovery of X-rays gave us new information in "flat form" on what was occurring inside the body. The introduction of Computerized Tomographic (CT) scanning in the 1970s improved the value of this data by changing how it was collected and how it could be rendered in multidimensional slices. Today's advances in medical imaging allow us to view massive quantities of imaging data in three-dimensional form. Such images are now being infused with intelligence to further improve their value.

Electronic Health Records (EHRs) were another breakthrough in how data is curated, stored, and used. They ushered in a new approach to making better use of information collected in the care process. The value proposition, however, has historically been in making data more accessible. Data was no longer tethered to a single, physical master copy of a medical record. Instead it became available in digital form to all with access privileges.

While the benefit of EHRs shifting information from paper to a digital format was important, this move was akin to freezing water. When frozen, water takes on a different form, but its underlying elements remain the same.

Today, a conservative estimate is that health and medical data is doubling every 24 months with total health data expected to swell to 2,314 exabytes in 2020. To put this in perspective, if all of this data were to be stored in a stack of tablet computers, it would create a tower of tablet computers 82,000 miles high.[9]

Equally important to understand is that the speed of data growth is accelerating. We'll soon be talking about health data being measured in zettabytes (ZB) and yottabytes (YB). To put this into perspective, if a byte of information is the equivalent of a single character, then a ZB would equal 1,000,000,000,000,000,000,000 bytes of information, which is roughly the equivalent of a hard drive that could store more than 34 trillion 3-minute MP3 songs.[10]

So, where is all of this data coming from? It's coming from traditional sources such as EHRs, imaging, labs, registration, and more. Equally important is a flood of data from new sources. These include remote monitoring, clinical surveillance, social and environmental data, and a host of biodata including genomics and proteomics. These new data sets are information rich and contribute to a much wider view of individual patients as well as populations of patients.

Despite the torrents of valuable data available, many organizations remain behind the curve in harnessing its use. For AI to create the value necessary to move health organizations forward there must be a recognition and actions that treat all data as a strategic asset.

Leadership is the key to success.

Whether you are a clinician or healthcare leader you're faced with an unrelenting set of challenges. These include expanding medical capabilities, constrained resources, staff shortages, and an increasingly diverse mix of patients and consumers whose needs only grow. Merely getting better with the tools we have is not going to deliver the results we need and that intelligent health consumers expect.

A tectonic shift in how health services are delivered is coming as AI allows technology to mimic human functions. As the roles between machines and humans begin to blur, it gives us the opportunity to reimagine the health consumer and patient experience while rethinking and reworking most aspects of clinical and operational workflows. In this regard, the critical difference between AI driving value in service of our missions and business objectives, or ending up as another expensive tech casualty littering the trail towards Intelligent Health Systems, is leadership.

As AI drives large-scale change and disruption successful leaders will need to become adept at leading their organizations in pursuing a dual strategy. This means both protecting and repositioning core service lines that exist today while actively investing in transformation activities that seed the new growth opportunities. More on this in Chapter 7.

This pursuit of "two journeys" sets an organization in a new direction while recognizing that a transition period is needed to accommodate the move to new processes and ways of doing business. Because dual transformations typically take years, there's no time to waste in getting started.

As AI will eventually change the nature of work and employment across virtually all jobs, your Chief Human Resources Officer will be every bit as important to the success of your AI strategy as your Chief Information Officer. They will help transition knowledge workers away from lower value repetitive work to focus on higher value activities, reduce the burden of labor intensive tasks, use AI to buffer human resource shortages, and help create data-driven cultures that become a competitive advantage. More on this in Chapter 8.

Governance and operating models will change to accommodate the AI-enabled organizations and spawn a host of issues as you delineate the role of clinicians versus intelligent machines. New types of legal and regulatory risks will arise that go beyond current data security and compliance issues. Your organization will need to be prepared to address things like AI bias and transparency. More on this in Chapter 11.

It's against this backdrop that AI holds the promise of fueling the creation of Intelligent Health Systems. From automating highly repetitive tasks to improving clinical decision making and empowering consumers, AI is already demonstrating its value in health organizations around the world (you'll hear more about these throughout the book).

This book is for anyone who believes that the provision of health and medical services is a noble cause and wants to better understand and apply AI as a force for positive change. In the end, the advent of AI in health as a move towards becoming an Intelligent Health Systems is as much a cultural and paradigm shift as it is a technology initiative.

Notes

1　Mihaela Porumb, Ernesto Iadanza, Sebastiano Massaro, Leandro Pecchia, A convolutional neural network approach to detect congestive heart failure, *Biomedical Signal Processing and Control Journal*, 2019.
2　Anne D'innocenzio and Tom Murphy, Walmart's Sam's Club Launches Health Care Pilot to Members, AP Business Writers, 2019, www.usnews.com/news/us/articles/2019-09-26/walmarts-sams-club-launches-health-care-pilot-to-members.
3　Creative destruction, Wikipedia, Accessed 2019, https://en.wikipedia.org/wiki/Creative_destruction.
4　The 2019 CitiusTech 'AI in Healthcare' Readiness Survey, Citiustech, 2019, www.citiustech.com/knowledge-hub/resource/perspective/402%5E$2019-CitiusTech-Survey-hosted-by-CHIME.
5　Ibid.
6　www.infosys.com/smart-automation/Documents/ai-healthcare.pdf.
7　Artificial Intelligence—Top 10 Applications in Healthcare, Global, 2018–2022, Frost and Sullivan, April 2019.
8　Weber Shandwick, AI-Ready or Not: Artificial Intelligence Here We Come!, www.webershandwick.com/news/article/ai-ready-or-not-artificial-intelligence-here-we-come.
9　Kenneth Corbin, How CIOs Can Prepare for Healthcare 'Data Tsunami', CIO, 2018, www.cio.com/article/2860072/how-cios-can-prepare-for-healthcare-data-tsunami.html.
10　Amy Smith, How Big Is a Petabyte, Exabyte, Zettabyte and Yottabyte? Top Ten Reviews, 2016, www.toptenreviews.com/how-big-is-a-petabyte-exabyte-zettabyte-or-a-yottabyte.

Chapter 2

The Rise of the Intelligent Health Consumer

"As in the earlier industrial revolutions, the main effects of the information revolution on the next society still lie ahead."

—Peter Drucker

The world is becoming more intelligent and mobile, thanks to the cloud, the Internet, and a cornucopia of Artificial Intelligence (AI)-enabled smart devices and apps.

Today 4 billion people are now connected to the Internet, and nearly all of them do so using mobile devices (92.6%). Every day, 85% of users (3.4 billion people) connect to the Internet and spend, on average, six-and-a-half hours online.[1]

Consumers are spending more time with less effort using an exponentially expanding range of AI-enabled apps to manage and enrich virtually all activities of daily living. In the time it takes to read this chapter, 100,000 consumers will order an Uber through its AI-enabled app on their smartphones. To service each customer request Uber will use AI to instantaneously predict rider demand. They will use AI to determine "surge pricing," calculate estimated time of arrival (ETA) for each ride, compute optimal pickup locations, and scan for credit card fraud.[2]

As riders are taken to their destinations (likely in a Prius) they will fill time using AI-driven apps on their smartphones. They will check a travel site that predicts which day will be the cheapest to buy tickets for an

11

upcoming vacation. They will Yelp to evaluate a company before giving it their business. They'll preorder dinner from their favorite restaurant app that makes intelligent suggestions based on its understanding of each family member's culinary likes and dislikes.

When they get home they will use smart devices and conversational AI to provide contextual interactions between the digital and physical worlds (Hey Cortana, remind me to talk to the product team lead tomorrow when I get to the office), direct requests for physical products and services (Alexa, order more laundry detergent), and drive social interactions (Hey Siri, call my brother with FaceTime).

Despite the cost reduction and benefits of AI to the activities of daily living, when it comes to healthcare these same consumers are paying a growing portion of their healthcare costs. Even if they're fortunate to be part of an employer-sponsored plan they'll shell out an average of $6,000 annually for a family's health insurance plan. That's just their share of the upfront premiums and doesn't include copayments, deductibles, and other cost-sharing fees once they need care.[3]

Beyond costs, intelligent consumers are hard-wired into the convenience of online banking, shopping, and an endless supply of free or low-cost business and personal apps. All of these allow them to make things happen on their terms. Their attitudes about healthcare choices and how much administrative complexity they want to endure are altered towards having the same expectations of doing things "smartly" on their terms.

Let's look at millennials for a moment. Those born between 1981 and 1996 are now the second largest generation among commercially insured Americans. And they're on track to become the largest generation in the near future.[4] Unlike older generations, millennials walk to the beat of a very different drum. Only 68% of millennials have a primary care physician, compared to 91% of Gen Xers.[5] They are less influenced by traditional marketing but are highly influenced by social media. They are twice as likely as other generations to take actions based on health advice via social media channels or online.[6]

Another key characteristic of the intelligent consumer is that self-service and on-demand customer service is not only accepted, it is expected. A large and growing portion of health consumers want, and expect, a quick answer or resolution to a question or problem. And unlike older generations, they don't want to make a phone call to get it.

The proliferation of AI is already ever-present in the average consumer's life and is transforming how they incorporate information, interfaces, and exchanges. They are driven by the desire to not only to simplify their lives but also to add flexibility and personalization into their increasingly demanding lives.

It is against this backdrop of desired efficiency, coupled with high deductible health plans requiring predeductible out-of-pocket spending, that you should ask the question of what experiences your organization will offer these empowered consumers when they have a health-related need for themselves or their families.

The Rise of Intelligent Health Systems

As the "connected health consumer" becomes the new norm, traditional health organizations will compete with new market entrants for mind share and market share of this important population. These market dynamics will lead to the emergence of Intelligent Health Systems.

So, what exactly is an Intelligent Health System? Simply put, an Intelligent Health System is an entity that leverages data and AI to create strategic advantages through the efficient provision of health and medical services across all touchpoints, experiences, and channels.

Intelligent Health Systems will take new approaches to overcome the age-old challenges of improving access, quality, effectiveness, and costs of health services. They will do this by being faster and smarter than similar organizations in making use of AI-enabling technologies, ubiquitous connectivity, and smart devices and systems.

From global non-governmental organizations (NGOs) and regional health systems to individual departments within a hospital or government-sponsored social service organization, Intelligent Health Systems will come in all sizes and forms. The defining characteristic will not be size but rather how they use data and AI to drive measurable change and improved outcomes at scale.

"An Intelligent Health System is an entity that leverages data and AI to create strategic advantages through the efficient provision of health and medical services across all touchpoints, experiences and channels."

Other characteristics that differentiate Intelligent Health Systems from traditional health organizations include:

- Blurring or eliminating historical care and service delivery boundaries by utilizing smart technologies like the internet of things (IOT), remote monitoring and wearables, virtual visits, virtual clinical assistants, and digital twins.
- Eliminating the traditional "partitions" between health and wellness services and medical interventions with the use of predictive capabilities to dramatically increase the proactive nature of monitoring and managing the health of individuals as well as the health of populations.
- New processes and workflow models supported by AI-driven automation that reduce the complexity of the medical bureaucracy that exists today. This will improve the consumer and patient experience.
- More effective and seamless provision of health and clinical services that are enabled through the automatic exchange of information across previously siloed data systems.
- Greater satisfaction and effectiveness of clinicians through the use of assistive intelligence that reduces administrative burden while increasing the real-time, predictive capabilities of structured and unstructured data from multiple sources to support the provision of evidence-based, patient-centered care.
- Intelligent forward-looking population analyses that guides future development and agile adjustments to planning and service delivery to more efficiently and accurately meet the needs of health consumers and patients.
- Turning smart consumer devices into powerful diagnostic, health and engagement tools by delivering seamless two-way connectivity to information and services considered useful and convenient to users.

As you consider your next moves on the path to becoming an Intelligent Health System, here are five things to consider.

Digital Transformation Is the On-Ramp for Intelligent Health

Health organizations of all sizes today are investing in various digital transformation efforts. Many see this move as a market strategy and differentiator. And while such investments are critical to future success, it's important to recognize that digital saturation is the new norm amongst consumers. Today every organization is investing in digital and AI technologies. As such, your organization's digital transformation effort is less of a strategy and more a "price of admission" to compete in the intelligent health arena.

Healthcare is in a unique place in the "post-digital" world. The industry is recognizing that digital must become part of everything it does. And while investments in social, mobile, analytics, and cloud (SMAC) technologies are progressing and demonstrating value, the health industry has not come as far in adoption maturity as other industries.

Today, innovative health leaders are looking at how their digital technology investments will power changes to both business models and service delivery in keeping with the new norms or the market. The future will be about full adoption of SMAC and embracing AI technologies to transform outcomes and ultimately change lives. Planning today for the postdigital world is critical as healthcare enterprises continue on their digital transformation journeys.

Emerging Intelligent Health Systems are changing the game and bypassing traditional health market strategies by making better use of data, and a growing array of AI-powered tools and apps to redefine how services are delivered. They are leveraging these assets as tools to better understand their customers and patients with a new depth of granularity and develop smartly efficient methods of providing health services to consumers on their terms.

Walgreens is a great example. They are pioneering new healthcare delivery models by leveraging cloud-enabled AI within their massive brick and mortar footprint (9,800 locations) and by providing a growing array of smart applications.

Their approach includes new in-store "digital health corners," telemedicine kiosks, and a digital marketplace called Find Care Now, which is a desktop and mobile app that allows consumers to find and access local and digital health services including neighborhood clinics and physician house calls. The Walgreens mobile app alone has been downloaded more than 50 million times and has 5 million active users a month.[7]

Even Walmart, the world's largest retailer, is getting into the business of health by combining its retail footprint with intelligent online tools to offer a growing array of primary and specialty services that were typically the purview of traditional provider organizations.[8]

If you are working in a traditional provider or payor organization, one of the top challenges is not whether your organization will become an Intelligent Health System but rather how you will keep up with the demands and expectations of those you seek to serve. If you don't… who will?

There Are No Swim Lanes in the Blue Ocean

The intelligent marketplace is not only changing consumer habits but also erasing historical industry boundaries and encouraging new players to enter the health market. The time when the healthcare could be delineated into categories like providers, payors, and retail health is giving way to a new market. It's being driven by those who seize opportunities to use their AI and data prowess to identify and curate new types of relationships with health consumers.

In the book *Blue Ocean Strategy*, authors W. Chan Kim and Renee Mauborgne present an analytical framework that fosters an organization's ability to systematically create and capture "blue oceans" – unexplored new market areas. It's an approach used by new entrants to the health market that focuses on solutions that are both exponentially more valuable to end users *while lowering costs*. The end goal for disruptors is to create new demand and capture uncontested market space in a way that makes the historical market players less relevant. The success of Netflix, Wikipedia, and Airbnb are all examples of blue ocean strategy.[9]

Take Amazon for example. They've set their sights on healthcare by creating a partnership with Berkshire Hathaway (an insurance and holding company) and JP Morgan Chase (a global financial services firm). Known as Haven, the stated goal of this new entity is to pool resources and expertise to explore ways to disrupt the current health market.[10]

On its own, Amazon announced the creation of Amazon Care. This pilot is initially focused on Amazon employees. They will have concierge level access to virtual and in-person care, an intelligent telemedicine app as well as follow-up visits and prescription drug delivery to a person's home or office.[11]

Not to be outdone, Walmart jumped into the health world with a bundled set of services for Sam Club members. This includes unlimited telehealth at one dollar per visit. This AI-driven service has patients first telling their symptoms to a chatbot or automated assistant. The information gathered then gets passed along to a clinician for diagnosis and treatment.[12]

Another example is pharma giant CVS acquiring healthcare insurer Aetna in a bid to expand its footprint into transforming healthcare delivery.

The Consumerization of Health

Many health consumers and patients are transforming from passive to active participants in taking charge of their healthcare delivery. They are doing this by using online review sites and social media to choose which doctor to see, skipping hospital and traditional physician office visits in favor of health clinics built into retail outlets or company-sponsored virtual visits. For example, according to a Rock Health study, 42% of millennials have used synchronous video telemedicine, compared to just a quarter of Gen Xers and under 5% of Baby Boomers.[13]

Look closely and you see that much of this movement is being powered by smart apps and intelligent consumer engagement activities delivered by organizations that have adopted a blue ocean strategy. This revamping of the patient experience is an early example of the market moving to reward those choosing to become an Intelligent Health System.

AI Is the New UI

In the world of software and digital solutions, the term User Interface, or UI, describes the way or manner in which a user engages or interacts with a system. Think about apps on your phone or computer that do this well. Now think about apps and websites that increase your blood pressure as you try and get something done with a UI that is neither intuitive, convenient, nor personalized. With this concept in mind, consider how easy or difficult your organizational interfaces make it for today's consumers to utilize your services.

It's a useful exercise to apply the UI concept to how patients and consumers interact with your organization today. How might the application of AI plus intelligent processes and systems be used to improve your organization's "UI" for patients, clinicians, and staff?

In the world today products, services, and surroundings are increasingly customized with data and AI to cater to the individual. The challenges and opportunities in healthcare are to reimagine the existing processes and touchpoints we run consumers, clinicians, and staff through every day.

Think about this the next time you're in the grocery store weighing the option of standing in line to have a human ring you up versus using the self-checkout kiosks. Even these options are rapidly becoming obsolete as companies like Amazon apply AI to create a better experience. *Amazon Go* is an intelligent system being piloted in Seattle that allows shoppers to download an app and then simply walk out of the store with the items in their cart or basket. Instead of making the checkout process more efficient they are using AI to eliminate it.[14] It's also interesting to note that Amazon now owns Whole Foods. Imagine the level of convenience and disruption if such technology is applied at scale.

In the hospitality world, the race is on for smart hotel rooms. Companies like Marriot are investing heavily in Intelligent rooms geared towards personalizing the experience of each guest. From smart mirrors, lighting, and showers to devices that provide customized conversational AI, the goal is to know or anticipate the needs of each guest and then autogenerate a personalized experience based on information stored in an app.[15]

Just as Amazon is using AI to eliminate the checkout process, what might health organizations do to rethink registration, admitting, and discharge processes? Whether an exam room in a clinic or an inpatient environment, can we take a lesson from hotel chains like Marriot in using AI to create a more personalized experience with the physical surroundings in which we see patients?

Employee Experiences Will Be as Important as the Customer Experiences

These dynamics of a more personalized experience for health consumers and patients also extend to clinicians, caregivers, and all staff who will have an array of smart machines and knowledge systems that free them of many tedious tasks and allow them to focus on practicing to the tops of their licenses.

As a new class of intelligent workers emerges, those that know how to leverage smart systems and workflows will be in high demand and likely short supply. Critical to market success is recognizing that what's happening on the inside of the organization is going to be seen and felt on the outside by health consumers. Creating and maintaining a great employee experience not only supports an improved experience for the intelligent health consumer but also reduces the chance of other health organizations stealing your best people.

Intelligent Health Is a New Journey

While many good things have come from the traditional ways in which health and medical services are provided today, the systems we have created are struggling to keep up with the needs and demands of a changing market. These systems are being overwhelmed by a set of complex challenges that produce inconsistent quality, unacceptable levels of harm, too much waste, and unsustainable costs.

Increasingly, many health leaders have a vision and aspiration for being better. And while everyone is early in their journey towards Intelligent Health Systems the market is beginning to take hold as innovative leaders leverage smart technologies with the goal of having every contact with consumers and interface with staff be simpler, smarter, and more efficient.

Just as having a website and using social media doesn't make your organization an Internet company, the use of AI and smart applications doesn't make an organization an Intelligent Health System. Becoming an Intelligent Health System sets a high bar for health leaders to clear when it comes to developing or changing core organizational competencies involving technology, data, people, and delivery mechanisms. Such systems will be built by those who are prepared to think differently about how AI will drive changes to clinical and operational processes along with a laser focus on improving the experience for consumers, clinicians, and staff.

THE DNA OF INTELLIGENT HEALTH SYSTEMS – AN INTERVIEW WITH HARRY PAPPAS, CEO, INTELLIGENT HEALTH ASSOCIATION

When it comes to seeing and understanding the rise of intelligent health, there are few people in the world with as much history and experience in its evolution as Harry P. Pappas, Founder and CEO of the Intelligent Health Association (IHA). As a global, technology-centric organization, the mission of IHA is to help drive the adoption and implementation of intelligent technologies throughout the health ecosystem. IHA does this through advisory and educational services to clinical and health leaders in the United States, Europe, and the Middle East.

"Smart technologies are already having a huge impact on consumer health and wellness habits," says Pappas. "As the complexities of healthcare delivery increase and the sophistication of health consumers in using smart technologies grows, there's an imperative for health organizations to quickly move towards the adoption of AI and intelligent solutions to keep pace. In some ways the market is getting out ahead of many traditional providers which creates both a threat and opportunity going forward."

With topics ranging from AI, virtual reality, 3D printing, and intelligent voice technologies, IHA is routinely interacting with clinical and health leaders to forge collaborative efforts that champion the incubation and adoption of intelligent solutions that improve the provision of health and medical services across the spectrum of care settings.

> In our experience, the single best predictor of the success of any intelligent health initiative is the level of understanding and participation of clinical and C-suite leaders. It's critically important that leaders get their minds around how intelligent health solutions change how work is done, how things are managed and how relationships with consumers are built and solidified.

When it comes to current uses of AI, IHA is seeing interest in, and working with, health organizations in the following areas:

- Internet of Health Things (IOHT): Use of intelligent wearable medical technology that helps patients and clinicians monitor vital signs and symptoms with machine learning built in to assess and predict variables important that help proactively manage health and intervention activities.
- Infrastructure optimization: While optimizing the management of expensive facilities is not as sexy as clinical use cases it's an area driving measurable value. Use cases range from the use of technologies to create smart buildings to elevators that learn usage patterns that are then used to improve throughput efficiencies.
- Conversational AI: The advent of chatbots and intelligence voice devices are gaining traction in the health arena. In the home they are increasingly being used as a way of engaging consumers in managing their health. Use cases include real-time information and support for managing weight and stress.

Notes

1 Connected Commerce, The Neilsen Company, 2018, www.nielsen.com/us/en/insights/reports/2018/connected-commerce-connectivity-is-enabling-lifestyle-evolution.html.
2 Mansoor Iqbal, Uber Revenue and Usage Statistics 2019, www.businessofapps.com/data/uber-statistics/#1.

3 John Tozzi, The Cost of Health Insurance for a Family Hits a Record, Passing $20,000 a Year, Los Angeles Times, 2019, www.latimes.com/business/story/2019-09-27/health-insurance-costs-surpass-20-000-per-year-hitting-a-record.

4 Millennial health trends found in report concern doctors, Pittsburgh Business Times, 2019, www.bizjournals.com/pittsburgh/news/2019/10/08/millennial-health-trends-found-in-report-concern.html.

5 Ibid.

6 Bill Coontz, The Millennial Mandate: How 'Generation Y' Behavior is Shaping Healthcare Marketing Strategy, MediaPost, www.mediapost.com/publications/article/253264/the-millennial-mandate-how-generation-y-behavio.html.

7 Heather Landi, Walgreens' CMO on the Retailer's Expanding Healthcare Role, Microsoft Partnership, FierceHealth, 2019, www.fiercehealthcare.com/tech/walgreens-cmo-talks-digital-healthcare-and-microsoft-partnership?mkt_tok=eyJpIjoiWlRSaE9XTTNaREUwT0RabCIsInQiOiJPVmhlSm9PS2NFTWRFRTYzV2gxWVRZMUV1RlpQS3Fiem84VHpwwaXN1N213U1h5UU5MY281azZCVkh0M1A2cXJKNDRDcEtGWm1hNkk3Z3RRHakdmOUorbFcxNnQ4MUh1bnJZT2JZXC81N3lcL3dIVWtTMW4zdHlkc0S1NiRmNEVGtsIn0%3D&mrkid=1009087.

8 Christina Farr, Walmart Tests Dentistry and Mental Care as it Moves Deeper into Primary Health, CNBC, 2019, www.cnbc.com/2019/08/29/walmart-is-piloting-health-clinic-at-walmart-health-in-georgia.html.

9 W. Chan Kim, Renée Mauborgne, Blue Ocean Strategy, Harvard Business School Publishing, 2015.

10 Angelica LeVito, Amazon's Joint Health-Care Venture Finally Has a Name: Haven, CNBC, 2019 www.cnbc.com/2019/03/06/amazon-jp-morgan-berkshire-hathaway-health-care-venture-named-haven.html.

11 Darrell Etherington, Amazon Launches Amazon Care, a Virtual and In-Person Healthcare Offering for Employees, TechCrunch.com, 2019, https://techcrunch.com/2019/09/24/amazon-care-healthcare-service/.

12 Anne D'innocenzio and Tom Murphy, Walmart's Sam's Club Launches Health Care Pilot to Members, AP Business Writers, 2019, www.usnews.com/news/us/articles/2019-09-26/walmarts-sams-club-launches-health-care-pilot-to-members.

13 Millennials are Leading the Way in Digital Health, Huffington Post, 2017, www.huffpost.com/entry/millennials-are-leading-the-way-in-the-adoption-of_b_59f4bd62e4b05f0ade1b57a9.

14 Nick Wingfield, Inside Amazon Go, a Store of the Future, New York Times, 2018, www.nytimes.com/2018/01/21/technology/inside-amazon-go-a-store-of-the-future.html.

15 Gary Diedrichs, The 'Smart' Hotel Room Race Is On, Smart Meetings, 2017, www.smartmeetings.com/technology/104502/smart-hotel-room-race.

Chapter 3

AI Is One Thing and Many Things

Alan Turing was an English mathematician, computer scientist and theoretical biologist who is considered to be the father of modern computer science. He formed the concept of algorithms and came up with the idea of a machine that was capable of computing anything that could be computed. His seminal work is the basis for the 2014 movie *The Imitation Game*. In this film, Turing is seen using an early form of computer science to crack the secret code of the Germans. His work saved lives and helped to end World War II.

And while Turing first put forward the notion of a universal machine capable of developing and using algorithms in the 1930s, it wasn't until the summer of 1956 that the world was first introduced to the term "AI." It was a situation that, should a movie be made, would more likely resemble a geeky version of *Animal House*.

John McCarthy was a young assistant professor of mathematics at Dartmouth College, who decided to hit up the Rockefeller Foundation for a grant to bring together mathematicians and scientists to explore emerging and fringe concepts of imbuing machines with "intelligence." With grant in hand, McCarthy invited a few dozen of his friends and top minds in math to a 2-month rolling nerd-party. The group checked in to the red-bricked Hanover Inn then sequestered itself on the top floor of the Dartmouth Math Department building. They would spend the summer in a continuous brainstorming session, which led to many of the concepts still used today.

From this gathering came the term "AI" along with many concepts of how machines could use language, form abstractions, and begin to solve problems previously reserved for humans. Many of the precepts formulated in the summer of 1956 remain relevant today. This includes concepts that formed the basis for things like Machine Learning (ML) and Natural Language Processing (NLP). In many regards, the rolling nature of what was started by Turing in the 1940s and McCarthy in the 1950s continues as we evolve in the capabilities and use of AI today (We'll learn more about the history of AI and its impact today in the next chapter).

AI Is One Thing and Many Things

The terms "Artificial Intelligence" and "AI" are often bandied about as if there is a singular definition that is universally understood. In reality, AI is not one technology. A simple Google search of "what is AI?" turns up 4.3 billion results.

AI is an umbrella term that includes multiple concepts and technologies used individually and in combination to add intelligence to computers and machines. For example, it is commonplace for the terms AI and Machine Learning (ML) to be used interchangeably. In reality, they are not the same. This misperception often causes confusion (as you will learn in this chapter, ML is usually classified as a subset of AI).

Equally important to understand is that the set of capabilities that fits within the term AI is evolving. As a health leader it is not imperative to be an expert in AI. It is, however, useful to understand the basics on which intelligent systems are built. To effectively plan and lead your organization's AI strategy it's important to have a general understanding of what it is. This includes having a framework for how the "components" and "capabilities" that exist can be used in defining, building, and managing intelligent systems. It is not necessary to know how AI actually works (though such knowledge never hurts). What is important to understand is what capabilities exist and how to put them to work in service of your organization's mission and goals.

When it comes to defining AI, there is generally broad agreement on what it is, but little or no standardization when it comes to organizing the components or building blocks of AI into a universally accepted taxonomy.

With this in mind, this chapter provides a working definition of AI as well as a nontechnical framework for understanding and applying these "AI building blocks" to your AI strategy. This book, nor this chapter, are not designed as a technical resource for AI. For those interested in going deeper on technical definitions and capabilities there are many great resources available.

Defining AI – General

Let's start with a simple but functional definition of AI:

> Artificial Intelligence (AI) is an area of computer science that emphasizes the creation of machines that work and react like humans. This means systems that have the ability to depict or mimic human brain functions including learning, speech (recognition and generation), problem-solving, vision and knowledge generation.

AI is a constellation of technologies that allow computers and machines to sense, comprehend, act, and learn. Unlike IT systems of the past that merely generated or stored data, the value of AI systems is that they can increasingly learn, adapt, and complete tasks in ways that are similar to a human being. In this regard AI imbues machines with intelligence. To understand and test this concept one can turn to what was posited by Alan Turing more than 60 years ago as a simple but effective definition of whether a machine is intelligent. The "Turing test" states that a machine can be considered "intelligent" if a human cannot distinguish the responses of a machine compared to responses from a human.[1]

AI Building Blocks

The general definition offered above is a descriptor for what AI *is*. The components of AI described below is the "how" part of the equation. These are the functional capabilities provided by AI today.

For the sake of providing a framework for understanding AI capabilities, let's take the broad definition noted above and break it down further into AI building blocks. A building block is an explicit component of AI that mimics a capability found in humans. We'll further separate the definition into two types of building blocks: Machine Learning and Cognitive Services.

Machine Learning (ML)

Ask anyone today what type of AI project they are working on and the most likely answer will be something they want to predict. The ability to predict things comes from **machine learning (ML),** which is a subset of AI. ML provides software, machines, devices, and robots with the ability to learn without human intervention or assistance or static program instructions.

Machine learning evolved from the study of pattern recognition and computational learning theory. The term was coined by AI pioneer J.A.N. Lee in 1959, who defined it as a "field of study that gives computers the ability to learn without being explicitly programmed.[2]"

Interestingly, Samuel is best known for his work with AI and computer gaming. If you think your kids spend too much time gaming, you can thank Samuel as he is credited with creating the world's first computer game. Known as the "Samuel Checkers-playing Program", it was among the world's first successful self-learning programs that demonstrated the fundamental concept of AI. Other things that were to come decades later, such as use of IBM Watson to be the best players at chess or the game show Jeopardy, have their origins rooted in Samuel's groundbreaking work.

Today, machine learning is at the forefront of making AI real in health-care. It's at the heart of our ability to predict things we care about. It's used to identify the root cause of quality problems, recommend treatment options to clinicians, drive smartphone apps for consumers, improve operational efficiencies, and more.

Machine learning-enabled processes rely on the development and use of computerized algorithms that "learn" from data sets rather than strictly following rule-based, preprogrammed logic. An **algorithm** is a mathematical model based on sample data, known as "training data."

Machine learning uses algorithms to identify patterns in the data and then make predictions from those patterns with a degree of certainty. Based on input data, machine-learning can improve its accuracy over time through a feedback loop and modify the approach it takes in the future—hence the term "learning."

It's important to understand that the "learning" part of "machine learning" is purely mathematical and has little to do with understanding what the algorithm has learned. This is different than when humans analyze data where we build an actual understanding of the data to a certain extent. We'll go deeper into understanding and applying the differences in what AI is good at versus humans in Chapter 5.

In spite of lacking deliberate understanding and being a mathematical process, machine learning can prove useful in many tasks. It provides many AI applications the power to mimic rational thinking, given a certain context when learning occurs by using the right data.

Within the general category of machine learning are various models used to create different types of algorithms. For example, supervised learning algorithms are a type of machine learning that involves direct human supervision and use labeled data to predict future outcomes after being trained based on past data. Unsupervised learning focuses on the use of data in an unguided fashion that has not been labeled, classified or categorized to complete a cluster analysis that looks for relevant patterns or trends within the data.

Reinforcement learning is the training of machine learning models to make a sequence of decisions by identifying patterns and making decisions with minimal human intervention. It focuses on developing a self-sustained system that, throughout contiguous sequences of trials and errors, improves itself based on the combination of labeled data and interactions with new data.

Even within these three models are many terms you may hear about. For example, neural networks are a form of supervised learning consisting of interconnected units (like neurons) that process information by responding to external inputs, relaying information between each unit. The process requires multiple passes at the data to find connections and derive meaning from undefined data.

Deep learning uses large neural networks with many layers of processing units, taking advantage of advances in computing power and improved training techniques to learn complex patterns in large amounts of data. Common applications include image and speech recognition.

With the use of ML, AI is increasingly good at being able to sense and predict things we care about. Like which patients are at high risk of readmissions, falls, or unexpected deterioration. It can help with predictions of which treatments may produce the best outcomes. It's already making diagnostic images more "intelligent."

There are many outstanding technical books and resources available to describe the various types and forms machine learning algorithms can take (linear regression, logic regression, decision tree, and decision forests) as well as the various languages and methodologies used to create them (R, Python, Lisp, to name a few). Unless you are a budding data scientist, it is sufficient to recognize that there are various types of machine learning models and algorithms. This diversity of the languages and models allows data scientists and developers to design an approach using various models and languages that best fit the type of problem to be solved.

EARLY INTERVENTION FOR PATIENTS AFFECTED BY COPD USING AI AND ML

Medical experts at one of the largest health boards in Europe are using ML to remotely monitor and treat people with life-threatening lung conditions in their own homes.

NHS Greater Glasgow and Clyde are using ML to predict pulmonary risk with the goals of improving care for patients suffering from Chronic Obstructive Pulmonary Disease (COPD). COPD is a group of lung conditions that cause breathing difficulties. The World Health Organization (WHO) forecasts COPD to become the third leading cause of death worldwide by 2030. Within the United Kingdom, COPD affects 1.2 million people and is the second most common cause of emergency hospital admissions and accounts for one in eight of all UK hospital admissions. As a result, it is also a key driver in rising NHS costs with each unplanned hospital trip costing about £6,000.[16]

The project is designed to improve quality and reduce emergency hospital admissions among high-risk COPD patients through the use of AI to help recognize patterns in a patient's condition and provide early warnings to aid intervention and prevention. It does this by remotely monitoring patients' symptoms, physiology, and treatment in the home with ML algorithms being used to detect or predict clinical deteriorations such as acute exacerbations of COPD.

Beyond monitoring and managing the health of individual citizens, the initiative is also designed to enable hospitals across Scotland to predict patterns in COPD admissions and estimate their length of stay, helping them to better manage resources. AI-guided predictive modeling and cloud-based decision support dashboards will enable focused patient–clinician communication, target clinical team's resources, and facilitate early activation of self-management and tiered COPD treatment interventions.

The project aligns closely with the ambitions set out in the recently published Scottish Government Digital Health and Care Strategy by supporting the shift of care into the community, reducing readmission rates, and empowering citizens to more effectively manage their own care.[17]

The COPD project initially involves 400 patients. The goal of better prediction and management of this initial trial group of patients is to improve health status, have patients more deeply engaged in monitoring and managing their health while reducing hospitalizations which equates to a potential cost saving of £1.2 million per year. The service also aims to reduce emergency hospital admissions per year. If this is scaled across 20% of the highest risk COPD patients, the potential NHS savings equates to £1.4 billion.[18]

Cognitive Services

Beyond the power of making predictions through machine learning, there are a growing number of applications or solutions that can be categorized as cognitive services. As the title implies these AI building blocks mimic specific human functions including perception (e.g., seeing, hearing), language, thinking, and learning.

Such functionality is available today and most often deployed through the use of an **"Application Programming Interface or API."** An API is a preset group of computer commands and protocols used by programmers to create software or interact with external systems. APIs provide developers with the ability to efficiently perform common operations without writing the code from scratch.

While the list of Cognitive Services is constantly evolving, here are the most common types of applications.

Computer Vision: It is a field of computer science that works on enabling computers to see, identify, and process images in the same way that human vision does. It then provides appropriate output to complete a task. Computer vision is a form of AI, as the computer must interpret what it sees and then perform appropriate analysis.

Vision services allow humans to gain insights from images, pictures, and video. These capabilities range from detecting faces in pictures, automated image analysis, text, or video moderation as well as person recognition. The goal of computer vision is not only to see but also process and provide useful results based on the observation. For example, the application of computer vision in healthcare ranges from detecting faces to aid in things like member verification and patient registration to clinical applications including autodetecting abnormalities in diagnostic and pathology images.

A fun example of computer vision at work is the website www.how-old.net, which allows users to select or upload an image of a person to then have computer vision and machine learning estimate the age of the person in the image.

COMPUTER VISION TO SCREEN FOR HAZARDOUS SKIN LESIONS

Vision intelligence is being used to help screen for skin lesions that are potentially cancerous. Today various smartphone apps are available to download that allow users to take a picture of a skin lesion to assess the likelihood of being a cancer concern.

In a recent study by the International Skin Imaging Collaboration (ISIC) and the MedUni Vienna, researchers also found that when it comes to the diagnosis of pigmented skin lesions, AI is better than humans. This database includes benign (moles, sun spots, senile warts, angiomas, and dermatofibromas) and malignant pigmented lesions (melanomas and other types of skin cancer).

When it came to comparing "man versus machine" results, researchers found that the best humans diagnosed 18.8 out of 30 cases correctly, while the best AI performance diagnosed 25.4 out of 30 cases correctly. The team says two-thirds of all participating AI algorithms were better than humans, and this result had been evident in similar trials during the past year.

They also mention that although the algorithms were superior in this experiment, this does not mean that the machines will replace humans in the diagnosis of skin cancer as there are many other factors beyond initial diagnosis.[22]

Knowledge Extraction: It allows for the identification, organization, and extraction of specific information and knowledge from large amounts of preexisting data and information. As the amount of data and information increases in healthcare the ability to extract and mine this data to acquire new knowledge becomes vitally important.

Knowledge extraction allows us to use massive quantities of data and information to look for patterns that humans simply don't have the ability or time to see.

To illustrate this point, researchers from the Lawrence Berkeley National Laboratory used machine learning to reveal new scientific knowledge hidden in old research papers. Using just the language in millions of old scientific papers, a deep learning algorithm was able to make new scientific discoveries by sifting through scientific papers for connections humans had missed. And while the experiment was focused on new discoveries in material science the process could just as easily be applied to other disciplines such as medical research and drug discovery.[3]

Speech: The speech component of AI is getting a lot of uptake in health-care today as it provides the ability to implement speech translation and recognition features into applications and workflows to make an automated process more human (understand what a human is saying). This area also provides the ability to convert text to speech and vice versa on-the-go to understand user intent and interact with patients and consumers.

Speech recognition has been around a while, but the AI-enhanced capabilities have brought the capabilities of machines to be on par with the speech and language capabilities of humans.

Language Understanding: Allows a computer application to understand what a person is saying and wants in their own words.

Natural Language Processing (NLP): NLP enables computers to derive computable and actionable data from text, especially when text is recorded in the form of natural human language (i.e., phrases, sentences, paragraphs). This technology allows humans to record information in the most natural method of human communication (narrative text) and then enables computers to extract actionable information from that text. NLP is also capable of analyzing the often-nonstandard grammatical constructions common in medical language. Natural language understanding (NLU) is a subset of NLP that uses reasoning, inference, and semantic searching to help clinicians make decisions and take action.[4]

Text Analytics: Provides NLP over raw text for sentiment analysis, key phrase extraction, and language detection.

Search: Search is one of the most important services for nearly every application or solution nowadays. In order to implement a search service, it is essential to provide the best possible results.

CHATBOTS – BRINGING CONVERSATIONAL AI TO HEALTHCARE

Chatbots are part of a growing trend of intelligent virtual assistants in health which are improving customer service, increasing patient engagement, automating repetitive tasks, and allowing staff to spend more time in higher-value customer service activities. From a friendly voice to a text box flashing a simple "how can I help," intelligent assistance comes in the form of smart speech and text applications.

According to Gartner, 25% of customer service and support operations are now integrating virtual customer assistant (VCA) or chatbot technology across all engagement channels, up from less than 2% in 2017.[11]

As more customers engage with health providers through digital channels, VCAs and chatbots are being implemented for handling customer requests on websites, mobile apps, consumer messaging apps, and social networks. All of this is being driven by improvements in NLP, ML, and intent-matching capabilities.

Organizations using these intelligent solutions report a reduction of up to 70% in call, chat, and/or email inquiries after implementing a VCA or chatbot, according to Gartner research. They also report increased customer satisfaction and a 33% saving per voice engagement.[12]

Today, healthcare chatbots are a mix of both patient-only and patient–clinician applications that connect the two groups: administrative and diagnosis and treatment-related activities.

In the world of health plans, consumers often don't want to wade through a website or app, and really don't want to make a call and hear, "Please continue to hold." They just want to type a question and get an answer.

To the rescue is a chatbot created by Premera Blue Cross, the largest health plan in the Pacific Northwest of the United States. Premera' s virtual assistant is called Scout and uses easy-to-understand, text-based chat to help customers quickly know where to get information on claims, benefits, and other services. Users can talk to it in a natural way and get answers back in a way consumers actually speaks. With an avatar of a serene blue owl, Premera Scout helps customers "self-serve" basic questions at any hour, while giving customer-service employees more time to handle complicated requests.[13]

Premera Scout is helping deliver better customer service to the health plan's 2 million customers in Washington and Alaska.

Fueled by advances in AI and the boom in messaging apps, chatbots take advantage of AI building blocks including speech, text, and natural language processing capabilities to streamline what is often a complex maze of tele-phone prompts and long wait times for talking to a human.

Another example of smart customer service is Quest Diagnostics, a com-prehensive clinical laboratory. As a Fortune 500 company Quest Diagnostics has about 45,000 employees and operates in the United States, United Kingdom, Mexico, and Brazil. Every year, tens of millions of adults are asked to contact Quest Diagnostics for healthcare-related services that range from routine blood work to complex genetic and molecular testing. In today's increasingly self-service healthcare industry, details such as where to go, when, and what to do beforehand are typically up to the patients to figure out for themselves.

The Quest chatbot helps people who visit the Quest Diagnostics website during call center hours find testing locations, schedule appointments, and get answers to nonmedical questions such as whether to fast before a blood draw or when to expect results. If the bot is unable to answer a question or the user gets frustrated, the bot will transfer the user, along with the context of the conversation, to a person who can help – all without having the user pick up the phone. Based on a user-experience survey, Quest found that about 50% of their clients would prefer to engage with a chatbot instead of a search box or the frequently asked questions feature on a website.[14]

Chatbots and conversational AI is creating a new form of patient engagement and customer service that can be personalized to the needs of the consumer while, as needed or requested, leveraging the skills and availability of staff to get involved to allow the experience to remain human-focused.

Here are some of the top areas where conversational AI is driving innovation and an improved consumer and patient experience.

Repetitive Customer Service Inquiries and Interactions: Chatbots are now supporting and supplementing staff in answering routine questions around registration, scheduling, benefits, and billing.

Patient Engagement and Care Coordination: Increasingly chatbots are being used in issuing reminders, scheduling appointments, and automating prescription refill requests.

The benefit of chatbots in patient engagement is the ability to provide advice and information for routine things like healthy lifestyle tips or specific reminders for those with specific conditions like diabetes (all of course under the direction of the clinician driving the care plan). Another example of its benefit in patient engagement is the ability to provide intelligent reminders for things like helping patients with when to take their pills.

For example, in the UK, a chatbot can be used to search volumes of health information from the National Health Service (NHS). This includes choices for healthcare advice and resources that support consumers reviewing conditions and treatment options.[15]

Chatbots are increasing in sophistication, which allows users to enter their symptoms via chat, view a list of related conditions, and through a series of prompts identify a patient's potential condition.

Triage: Whether it's getting a consumer to the right person to answer a question or helping in the gathering of information to get to the root of a patient medical problem, AI-powered chatbots are creating a more efficient process for clinicians and consumers.

The goal of using chatbots and virtual assistant is to help clinical and operational staff optimize their time while putting more information in the hands of patients and consumers. In the end, this intelligent self-service option helps to drive better outcomes and reduce costs.

Applying AI Building Blocks

The AI "building blocks" described above are often used in combination and deployed in a variety of ways with other technologies (like sensors) to drive value in automating or augmenting work heretofore done by humans.

AI is sometimes classified by the level of sophistication or type of use. For example, **Narrow AI** (Artificial Narrow Intelligence or ANI) is good at performing a single task, such as predicting which patient is likely to be a no-show for an appointment. AI components like machine learning, computer vision, and natural language processing are currently in this stage. As such narrow AI is a bit like a digital idiot savant, it excels at one particular type of task within a limited context but isn't able to take on tasks beyond what it was designed to do. Even when pushing the boundaries of today's AI, most everything being done is through Narrow AI. For example, self-driving car technology is still considered ANI, or more precisely, a coordination of several narrow AIs[5].

Understanding that almost all AI deployed today is considered "narrow AI" is something we'll build on in the next chapter, as creating value is heavily dependent on understanding how to leverage and balance the capabilities of AI with the unique capabilities of your human teammates.

General AI (also known as Artificial General AI or AGI) is the type of AI that can understand and reason across its environment as a human would. General AI has always been elusive. This category of AI is where many organizations aspire to be someday (e.g. IBM's Watson), but any true form of this is not likely on the short-term horizon.

As you will learn in the next chapter, humans might not be able to process data as fast as computers, but they can think abstractly and plan, and can solve problems based on their experience and creativity. These factors, which are vitally important in delivering health services, are not found in the realm of what computers can replicate today nor likely anytime soon.

Finally, there is another category known as **Super Intelligence** (Artificial Super Intelligence or ASI) that is a level of computer sophistication where machines become smarter than the humans that create them. This is the stuff that becomes fodder for science fiction movies. It's also the type of AI you occasionally here people like Elon Musk waxing over as they ponder the dangers to mankind should we reach this level of AI capability.

For now, recognize that pretty much everything being done today falls into the Narrow AI category. Investments that are being made in the tech industry are designed to move systems closer to the General AI category.[6]

Here are some of the common ways AI is packaged and deployed today:

AI Apps: Web or mobile applications are infused with AI capabilities, such as vision, language, or ML. For example, AI is pervasive in our daily lives. From anonymized data from smartphones and other data, AI analyzes the speed and movement of traffic at any given time to predict when you will reach your destination and the best route to do so. As you make an online transaction with your credit card, AI is running in the background to monitor and predict whether the charge is fraudulent. When it comes to health, thousands of consumer health apps help monitor body functions, provide alerts for various health indicators, or guided recommendations on everything from nutrition to maintaining emotional and mental wellness.

Bots and Conversational AI: A bot is an automated application used to perform simple and repetitive tasks that are often time consuming for a human to perform. **Conversational AI** makes use of speech and language building blocks to automate communications and create personalized customer experiences that are scalable.

With consumers increasingly looking to access information on demand, the use of bots and conversational AI provide short and high value interactions with customer and staff through task automation and automated workflows. The goal in the use of Bots and Conversational AI is to improve the customer experience while reducing the need for lower-value human interactions.

In one survey of consumers nearly 70% saw chatbots as the best way to get instant answers to their questions and over one-fifth (21%) saw chatbots as the easiest way to contact a company.[7]

Intelligent IoT: The Internet of Things (IoT) is a network of Internet-connected devices that communicate embedded sensor data to the cloud for centralized processing. These sensors can be embedded in everyday items such as cell phones, digital weight scales, or wearable health and medical devices; or they could be components of larger machines and systems such as medical imaging or lab systems.

The introduction of intelligence with IoT enables health organizations to reimagine existing services or create new types of services that cut across historical care settings. Intelligent IoT also allows for the ability to improve operational efficiencies in areas that include smart remote patient monitoring or improved predictive maintenance of equipment and facilities.

IoT IN ACTION: AN ECG ON YOUR WRIST

There's a new breed of wearables emerging making it easier for people to continuously monitor their hearts with medical-grade devices.

While fitness trackers are popular among the "quantified-self" crowd, they aren't serious medical devices. Variables such as an intense workout or a loose band can affect the sensor reading your pulse. But an electrocardiogram (ECG), the kind doctors use to diagnose abnormalities before they cause a stroke or heart attack, requires a visit to a clinic, and people often fail to take the test in time.

ECG-enabled smart watches, made possible by new regulations and innovations in hardware and software, offer the convenience of a wearable device with something closer to the precision of a medical one. While standard fitness trackers typically employ a single sensor, a real ECG has 12. And no wearable can yet detect a heart attack as it's happening.

A number of IoT wearable devices are now receiving clearance for use that can detect things like atrial fibrillation (AFib), a frequent cause of blood clots and stroke. Worldwide more than 33.5 million people have AFib.[19] In the United States more than 750,000 hospitalizations occur each year because of AFib and contribute to nearly 130,000 deaths each year.[20]

At the moment, even people at risk for AFib with the best access to care get only two or three ECGs a year. Preventive screening through wearables could if widely implemented, potentially save thousands of lives. In addition to the monitoring work underway is a move to use deep learning algorithms with the data coming from wearables and look for new ways of using it. Apple and Johnson and Johnson partnered recently to a study that screens for stroke risk. And AliveCor's software developed in conjunction with the Mayo Clinic has been granted accelerated clearance to use deep learning on ECGs to screen for hyperkalemia, (elevated potassium levels in the blood) that puts people with kidney disease at risk for arrhythmia and death.[21]

Intelligent Robots: According to a study by Accenture, robot-assisted surgery is estimated to produce $40 billion in near-term value to health organizations.[8] With the help of AI, robots can use data from past operations to guide surgeons to improve existing surgical techniques and reduce the invasive nature of some surgeries. One study of the use of smart robotics in orthopedic surgeries resulted in five times fewer complications.[9]

Looking ahead, heart surgeons are now being assisted by a miniature mobile robot known as HeartLander, which facilitates minimally invasive therapy to the surface of a beating heart. Under the control of a physician, the **robot** enters the chest through an incision below the sternum and then autonomously navigates to the specified location on the heart to administer the therapy.[10]

Notes

1 Stuart J. Russell, Peter Norvig. *Artificial Intelligence: A Modern Approach* (3rd ed.). Upper Saddle River, NJ: Prentice Hall. ISBN 978-0-13-604259-4, 2009.
2 J.A.N. Lee, Arthur Lee Samuel, Computer Pioneers, IEEE Computer Society, https://history.computer.org/pioneers/samuel.html.
3 Vahe Tshitoyan, Unsupervised word embeddings capture latent knowledge from materials science literature, *Nature*, 2019, www.nature.com/articles/s41586-019-1335-8.epdf?referrer_access_token=gjs4tfb7-T50BFnuqtYx5N RgN0jAjWel9jnR3ZoTv0P9QxlcO86f_GXZRxwYijrqa11Mx55SgniZXv55YKOR_ sn816NK2x0O46Vim16XrS-SjyP9GMXeDQinUN75ES6enlxK__ J5UabR6JdgR19bZSVLL5ZsK8146qMcipEbItW65C8aSk29Q_BfrKz4Gb5-kjz 3m7dIaoRxs3e1I6qW4022QZ6aZMaOPxlATK7OOqj8lrhj- yufvROMPdStMZjAEK-efja6SfW5n-6xhZuV3zQTFR_u132mC6hkt8Zqp29_ su0pmsC0jrneuemHnqg8&tracking_referrer=www.vice.com.
4 Laura Bryan, MS, CHDS, AHDI-F, With Natural Language Processing You Can Have Your Cake and Eat It Too, HIMSS, 2019, www.himss.org/news/natural-language-processing-you-can-have-your-cake-and-eat-it-too.
5 Ben Dickson, What is Narrow, General and Super Artificial Intelligence, TEchTalks, 2017, https://bdtechtalks.com/2017/05/12/what-is-narrow-general-and-super-artificial-intelligence/.
6 Dean Van Nguyen, Elon Musk Calls Artificial Intelligence 'Our Biggest Existential Threat', Silicon Republic, 2014, www.siliconrepublic.com/machines/elon-musk-calls-artificial-intelligence-our-biggest-existential-threat.
7 2017 Chatbot Survey, Ubisend, 2017, www.ubisend.com/insights/2017-chatbot-report.
8 Matt Collier, Artificial Intelligences-Healthcare's New Nervous system, Accenture, 2017.
9 Brian Kalis, Matt Collier, Richard Fu, 10 Promising AI Applications in Health Care, *Harvard Business Review*, 2018, https://hbr.org/2018/05/10-promising-ai-applications-in-health-care.

10 HeartLander, Carnegie Mellon University Robotics Institute, 2016, www.ri.cmu. edu/project/heartlander/.

11 Gartner Says 25 Percent of Customer Service Operations Will Use Virtual Customer Assistants by 2020, Gartner Inc. 2018, www.gartner.com/en/ newsroom/press-releases/2018-02-19-gartner-says-25-percent-of-customer-service-operations-will-use-virtual-customer-assistants-by-2020.

12 Ibid.

13 Vanessa Ho, Skip the Hold Music and Meet Premera Scout, a Chatbot That Helps You with Health Care, Microsoft Blog, 2018, https://news.microsoft.com/ transform/premera-scout-chatbot-helps-with-health-care/.

14 John Roach, Microsoft Service Helps Healthcare Organizations Develop and Deploy Virtual Health Assistants, Microsoft Blog, 2019, https://blogs.microsoft. com/ai/microsoft-healthcare-bot-service/.

15 Kumba Sennaar, Chatbots for Healthcare – Comparing 5 Current Applications, Emerj.com, 2019, https://emerj.com/ai-application-comparisons/ chatbots-for-healthcare-comparison/.

16 NHS Greater Glasgow & Clyde is Monitoring COPD Patients with Wearables, NSTech, 2019, https://tech.newstatesman.com/cloud/nhs-greater-glasgow-clyde.

17 Scotland's Digital Health and Care Strategy, The Scottish Government, 2018, www.digihealthcare.scot/wp-content/uploads/2018/04/25-April-2018-SCOTLANDS-DIGITAL-HEALTH-AND-CARE-STRATEGY-published.pdf.

18 Doctors Are Using Technology to Help Patients with a Serious Lung Disease Get Treatment in Their Homes, Microsoft News Centre UK, 2019, https://news. microsoft.com/en-gb/2019/03/26/doctors-are-using-technology-to-help-patients-with-a-serious-lung-disease-get-treatment-in-their-homes/.

19 Atrial Fibrillation: Facts, Statistics, and You, Healthline, 2018, www.healthline. com/health/living-with-atrial-fibrillation/facts-statistics-infographic.

20 Ibid.

21 Don Hon, Wristwatch Heart Monitors Might Save Your Life—and Change Medicine, Too, *MIT Technology Review*, 2019, www.technologyreview. com/s/612929/wristwatch-heart-monitors-might-save-your-lifeand-change-medicine-too/.

22 Phillip Tschandi PhD et al., Comparison of the accuracy of the human readers versus machine-learning algorithms for pigmented skin lesion classification: An open, web-based, international, diagnostic study, *The Lancet Oncology*, 2018, www.thelancet.com/journals/lanonc/article/PIIS1470-2045(19)30333-X/fulltext#.

Chapter 4

From Gods to Geeks –
A Brief History of AI

The present purpose the artificial intelligence problem is taken to be that of making a machine behave in ways that would be called intelligent if a human were so behaving.

—John McCarthy

Citation from 1955 funding proposal to the Rockefeller Foundation where the term "Artificial Intelligence" was first used.

While Artificial Intelligence (AI) is a hot topic today, its history and intellectual roots can be traced as far back as Greek mythology. Here's a brief history of how it started leading up to its use today.

Basic concepts for what AI is today can be traced back to ancient times and Greek mythology. For example, the story of Hephaestus, the god of smiths, is about a blacksmith who manufactured mechanical servants. The story of Talos introduces and incorporates the idea of intelligent robots. Interestingly, the term "robot" would not be coined until 1925 when it was first used by Czech writer Karel Čapek in his play Rossum's Universal Robots.

In the 1500s, King Philip II of Spain could have been considered a "multitasking" ruler as he was also the king of Portugal, Naples, and Sicily. His beloved son became ill and neared death. Upon his unexpected recovery, the king commissioned the development of a mechanical monk so that he might automate the offering of continuous prayers. This might be considered an early "chatbot."

In the 1600s, philosopher Rene Descartes pondered the possibility that machines would one day think and make decisions. He also identified a division between machines which might one day learn about performing one specific task and those which might be able to adapt to any job. Today, this categorization is known as Narrow AI and General AI.[1]

In the 1700s, *Gulliver's Travels* was published by Jonathan Swift, which included a description of a strange little machine called the "Engine." The book notes that by using this device "the most ignorant person at a reasonable charge, and with a little bodily labour, may write books in philosophy, poetry, politicks, law, mathematicks, and theology, with the least assistance from genius or study." This sounds strangely like current discussions on the use of technology to augment the skills and expertise of knowledge workers today.

Around the same time, Thomas Bayes, an English nonconformist theologian and mathematician became the first to use probability inductively and established a mathematical basis for probability inference. In essence he defined a means of predicting the probability of an event occurring in the future based on the frequency by which an event occurred in prior trials. Known as Bayesian inference, this framework for reasoning about the probability of events went on to become the leading approach to machine learning.

In the 1800s, Ada Lovelace, the daughter of Lord Byron, became well known as an English mathematician and writer. As a teenager, she was befriended by Charles Babbage who was a preeminent mathematician, philosopher, and inventor who originated the concept of a digital programmable computer.[2] Based on her experiences with Babbage, Lovelace was the first to recognize and write about how computing machines had application beyond pure calculation noting that machines in the future "might compose elaborate and scientific pieces of music of any degree of complexity or extent."[3]

She went on to write and publish the first algorithm intended to be used on the mechanical computer that Babbage had designed, thereby making her possibly the first known computer programmer.

While biohacking is seen as a futuristic trend today, the most well-known fictional characterization of it occurred when Mary Shelley published in 1818 her first edition of Frankenstein, a timeless horror story that explores the ethical issues of creating artificial life.

And while contemporaries like Elon Musk and the late Stephen Hawking are known for sounding the alarm on how intelligent computers might surpass humans to take over the world, their concerns have their roots on the same speculation going back to 1863. It was English author Samuel Butler who published a piece called "Darwin among Machines," which first raised the issues that machines were a kind of "mechanical life" undergoing constant evolution, and that eventually machines might supplant humans as the dominant species.

The 1900s was a time when AI was given a face and began moving into the mainstream of science and society.

In the summer of 1914 a great deal of excitement was generated when an autonomous machine capable of playing chess made its debut at the University of Paris. Considered by some to be the world's first computer game, El Ajedrecista (the chess player), was a fully automated machine that was able to play chess without any human guidance.

In 1935 at Cambridge University, Alan Turing conceived the principle of the modern computer. He described an abstract digital computing machine consisting of a limitless memory and a scanner that moves back and forth through the memory, symbol by symbol, reading what it finds and writing further symbols. Turing went on to propose the possibility to have machines operating on and modifying their own programs noting that "What we want is a machine that can learn from experience," adding that the "possibility of letting the machine alter its own instructions provides the mechanism for this."[4]

It was in the 1940s when scientists from a variety of fields (mathematics, psychology, engineering, economics, and political science) began to imagine and research the possibility of imbuing machines with intelligence. It was World War II that brought forth the value of such an idea. The war was taking a devastating toll on people and countries around the globe. The Allied forces have been intercepting and manually decoding encrypted messages from the German forces when, at some point, messages being intercepted were encoded with a totally different method that could not be cracked.

The need to decipher this vital intelligence as rapidly as possible led to the development and mission-critical use of a new type of machine capable of automating work being done by cryptanalysts. At the time Turing was a leading cryptanalyst at the Government Code and Cypher School at Bletchley Park. In collaboration with other leading minds at the time Turing led efforts to create the first fully functioning digital computer in 1943.

Known as Colossus, this behemoth prototype required 1,600 vacuum tubes, was unreliable and required constant effort to keep its high-speed paper tapes from breaking. Those who knew of Colossus were prohibited by the Official Secrets Act from sharing their knowledge. It wasn't until the 1970s that details came to light about how electronic computations had been successfully used to help win the war. Historians for the British government estimated that the war in Europe was shortened by at least 2 years as a result of the signals intelligence operations, in which Colossus played a major role.[5]

The use of what would eventually become known as AI during World War II was a major breakthrough in demonstrating the mission-critical nature of intelligent machines and is likely the starting point for the nascent fields of data science and information technology.

Some of the early concepts and work in conceptualizing intelligent machines actually came from clinical research. For example, during the 1930s and 1940s research in the area of neurology showed that the brain was a network of neurons that burst in all-or-nothing impulses.

Walter Pitts and Warren McCulloch were professors at the Massachusetts Institute of Technology (MIT) and early AI pioneers who took key concepts from clinical research to speculate on how "artificial neurons" might allow machines to perform simple logical functions. In 1943 the duo published a seminal paper in scientific history titled "A Logical Calculus of Ideas Immanent in Nervous Activity".[6] This paper proposed the first mathematical model of a neural network. It wasn't until 1951 that the first artificial neural network was built using 3,000 vacuum tubes to simulate a network of 40 neurons (the device was known as the Stochastic Neural Analog Reinforcement Calculator or SNARC).[7]

Today, neural networks form the basis of what is known as deep learning and is a means of doing machine learning where a computer learns to perform tasks by analyzing training examples. Many of the image recognition systems used in healthcare and other industries today make use of neural networks.

NEURAL NETWORKS THAT DETECT HEART FAILURE FROM A SINGLE HEARTBEAT

Imagine the ability to utilize AI to detect heart failure from a single heartbeat with 100% accuracy. Sound futuristic? It may be closer than you think, thanks to the early work on neural networks pioneered in the 1940s by MIT professors Walter Pitts and Warren McCulloch.

Congestive heart failure (CHF) is a chronic progressive condition that affects 26 million people worldwide and is increasing in prevalence.[8] Along with its high prevalence comes the need for more efficient detection processes.

According to a recent report published in the *Biomedical Signal Processing and Control Journal* a group of researchers from the Universities of Surrey (UK), Warick (UK), and Florence (Italy) developed and applied Convolutional Neural Networks (CNN) to ECG data sets. A CNN is a hierarchical neural network that recognizes patterns and structures in data. Researchers applied the CNN to ECG data sets that included subjects with CHF as well as healthy, nonarrhythmic hearts. In applying this to just one heartbeat researchers report that they were able to detect whether a person had heart failure.[9]

Today, existing methods of detecting CHF typically rely on evaluating heart rate variability which is time-consuming and prone to errors. Combining the use of advanced signal processing with neural networking researchers reports that they were able to predict heart failure with 100% accuracy.

In the United States alone there are 550,000 new cases of CHF a year and, on its own, generates more hospitalizations alone than all cancers combined.[10] The eventual adoption and use of such AI-enabled applications allow clinicians to make a more significant societal impact with patients benefiting from early and more efficient diagnoses.

It was 1956, and as people were shuffling back to work from their Christmas and New Year's holidays swapping stories of their time off, Herbert A. Simon and Allen Newell had a Christmas break story that would top them all. "Over the Christmas holiday," Dr. Simon famously blurted to one of his classes at Carnegie Institute of Technology, "Al Newell and I invented a thinking machine."[11]

While the idea of a digital computer was still in its infancy, researchers, philosophers, and others were talking developing a crude device as an "electronic brain." As others mused over such concepts, these two young Carnegie Tech scientists used their holiday to work through their own version of a thinking machine and put it in a form that could be programmed into a computer.

Dr. Simon would eventually go on to pioneer "heuristics," or rules of thumb, that humans use to solve geometry problems and that could be programmed into a computer. This work earned him a Nobel prize. Dr. Newell went on to develop a programming language that could mimic human memory processes.

Later that year a summer conference organized by John McCarthy (noted in Chapter 3) brought together top minds at Dartmouth College to specifically focus on the idea of imbuing machines with intelligence. The proposal for the conference included the assertion that "every aspect of learning or any other feature of intelligence can be so precisely described that a machine can be made to simulate it."[12] It was from this gathering that AI gained its name and mission and is considered by many as the official "birth of AI" as it legitimized the field as a formal scientific discipline. Those who attended would become the leaders of AI research for decades.

In the period between the late 1950s and the early 1960s came a torrent of theories and experiments, which both moved AI forward and brought it into the public and government spotlight.

In 1958, John McCarthy developed a programming language known as Lisp. It went on to become the most popular programming language used in AI research. While Lisp has changed since its early days, it is still in use today.

In 1959, Arthur Samuel, considered as a pioneer in the gaming world, coined the term "machine learning," in a journal article, outlining how a computer could be programmed to play a better game of checkers that the person who wrote the program, demonstrating that the computers could be able to master a process of learning. That same year another study is published describing a process by which computers could recognize patterns that have not been specified in advance. Yet another study reported on a program for solving problems by manipulating sentences in formal languages with the ultimate objective of creating programs "that learn from their experience as effectively as humans do."[13]

By 1961, early forms of AI were making their way into commercial use. In this year, the first industrial robot called Unimate began working on an assembly line in a General Motors plant in New Jersey.[14] At the same time the space race was getting underway, which meant that major investments were now going to universities and private labs to expand the capabilities and reach of this new science.

In 1964, ELIZA, the world's first chatbot was created at the MIT AI Lab to demonstrate basic communications between humans and machines. Named after a character from George Bernard Shaw's play Pygmalion, ELIZA is an example of an early natural language computer program. In its most famous use case, it simulated a Rogerian psychotherapist to respond with nondirectional questions to user inputs.

With the progress being made in making machines "intelligent" came many exaggerated claims as to its impact on the world outside of the laboratory. In their enthusiasm many AI leaders put forward wild predictions around how machines as intelligent as humans would exist within a decade. Anxious to usher in the new world, governments and private corporations invested millions to make the vision come true. In the end, both leaders and funders of the day had grossly underestimated the difficulty of achieving this vision and the amount of time and money that would be required.

As the speed and number of "AI-firsts" accelerated, the world was about to learn of another first, which is now known as the technology "hype cycle."

Today we better understand that patterns exist in the creation and adoption of new technology. The best depiction of this is **Gartner's Hype Cycle,** which is a graphical depiction of a common pattern that arises with each new technology or other innovation. The five phases in the Hype Cycle are Technology Trigger, Peak of Inflated Expectations, Trough of Disillusionment, Slope of Enlightenment, and Plateau of Productivity.[15]

As the 1970s came around AI was about to go into the phase Gartner describes as the "Trough of Disillusionment." Criticism was growing about how AI researchers had overpromised and underdelivered products or solutions that would have a real-world impact. With enthusiasm for AI having spiraled out of control for the past two decades what followed in the 1980s was a period of greatly reduced funding and interest in AI research. This eventually became known as the "AI Winter" as the billion-dollar AI industry began to collapse.

From this point until a resurgence of interest and investing, beginning in the mid-2000s, many top computer scientists and software engineers were deliberate in avoiding the term "artificial intelligence" for fear of being viewed as "wide-eyed dreamers.[16] In order to receive funding, advances continued during this period, but many initiatives were packaged under different names such as informatics or data science.

While it was roughly a decade ago that the AI resurgence began, the impetus for a new awakening came in 1991 when Tim Berners-Lee, a researcher for the Center for European Nuclear Research (CERN), put the world's first website online and published the workings of the hypertext transfer protocol (HTTP). Up until this point, computers have been connecting to share data for decades, mainly at educational institutions and large businesses.

The arrival of the worldwide web was the catalyst for society at large to plug itself into the online world. As millions of people from every part of the world began getting connected new types of data were being developed and shared at a previously inconceivable rate. With data being the fuel, which AI runs on, a new chapter in its growth began.

In 2007 a team from Princeton University successfully assembled ImageNet, a large database of annotated images designed to be used in visual recognition software.[17] Over the years an annual competition known as the ImageNet challenge pitted researchers from around the world in developing algorithms that can recognize and describe a library of 1,000 images. Since its launch in 2010 the accuracy rate of the winning algorithm jumped from 71.8% to 97.3%. In 2015 judges declared that computers could identify objects in visual data more accurately than humans.[18]

In 2009 Google started a secret project to develop a driverless car. In 2014, it became the first autonomous vehicle to pass a U.S. state self-driving test. In the same year, computer scientists at Northwestern University developed a program that wrote sport news stories without human intervention.

In 2011 IBM enlists Watson, its cognitive computing platform, to compete in the popular television show Jeopardy! and defeats two former champions. IBM uses this public relations event to launch Watson as a major move to bring AI to healthcare.[19]

Not to be outdone, Google showcased its AI prowess by training an algorithm designed to beat what is known commonly as the world's most complex game; Go. Google's algorithm, called AlphaGo, first beat the European Go champion in 2015, then the Korean Go champion in 2016 and finally the World Go champion in 2017.[20] In 2019 the GO World Champion Lee Se-dol retired from professional play after claiming artificial intelligence is "an entity that cannot be defeated".[21]

In 2016 Microsoft made a major breakthrough in speech recognition, demonstrating for the first time that a computer could recognize the words in a conversation as well as a person does.[22]

In 2017 the AI Now Institute was launched at New York University (NYU) to research and study the social implications of AI. Its work focuses on four core domains including rights and liberties, labor and automation, bias and inclusion, and safety and critical infrastructure.

Today we are inundated with news of new breakthroughs and capabilities that are moving from the lab and research centers into everyday use. As we look ahead at the possibilities and applications in our professional and personal lives it's worth reflecting how we are standing on the shoulders of those who came before us.

Notes

1 Bernard Marr, The Most Amazing Artificial Intelligence Milestones So Far, *Forbes*, 2018, www.forbes.com/sites/bernardmarr/2018/12/31/the-most-amazing-artificial-intelligence-milestones-so-far/#35fe52ef7753.

2 Brian Jack Copeland, (18 December 2000). *The Modern History of Computing (Stanford Encyclopedia of Philosophy)*. Metaphysics Research Lab, Stanford University. Retrieved 1 March 2017.

3 Ada Lovelace, Wikipedia, accessed 2019, https://en.wikipedia.org/wiki/Ada_Lovelace.

4 Jack Copeland, A Brief History of Computing, AlanTuring.net, Accessed 2019, www.alanturing.net/turing_archive/pages/Reference%20Articles/BriefHistofComp.html.

5 Ibid.

6 A logical calculus of the ideas immanent in nervous activity, *Bulletin of Mathematical Biology*, 1990, www.sciencedirect.com/science/article/pii/S0092824005800060.

7 Gil Press, A Very Short History of Artificial Intelligence (AI), *Forbes*, 2016, www.forbes.com/sites/gilpress/2016/12/30/a-very-short-history-of-artificial-intelligence-ai/#4ab002866fba.

8 Global Public Health Burden of CHF, *Cardiac Failure Review*, 2017, www.cfrjournal.com/articles/global-public-health-burden-HF.

9 Mihaela Porumb, Ernesto Iadanza' Sebastiano Massaro, Leandro Pecchia, A convolutional neural network approach to detect congestive heart failure, *Biomedical Signal Processing and Control Journal*, 2019, www.sciencedirect.com/science/article/pii/S1746809419301776.

10 Heart Failure Statistics, Emory Healthcare, 2019, www.emoryhealthcare.org/heart-vascular/wellness/heart-failure-statistics.html.

11 Byron Spice, Over the Holidays 50 Years Ago, Two Scientists Hatched Artificial Intelligence, Post-Gazette.com, 2006, http://old.post-gazette.com/pg/06002/631149-96.stm. Read more: http://old.post-gazette.com/pg/06002/631149-96.stm#ixzz5yZBgKjhm.

12 John McCarthy, Marvin Minsky, Nathan Rochester, Claude Shannon, 31 August 1955, A Proposal for the Dartmouth Summer Research Project on Artificial Intelligence, retrieved 16 October 2008.

13 Gil Press, A Very Short History of Artificial Intelligence (AI), *Forbes*, 2016, www.forbes.com/sites/gilpress/2016/12/30/a-very-short-history-of-artificial-intelligence-ai/#4ab002866fba.

14 Ibid.

15 IT Glossary, Gartner, accessed 2019, www.gartner.com/it-glossary/hype-cycle.

16 Markoff, John, Behind Artificial Intelligence, a Squadron of Bright Real People, *The New York Times*, 2005, www.nytimes.com/2005/10/14/technology/behind-artificial-intelligence-a-squadron-of-bright-real-people.html.

17 ImageNet, Wikipedia, accessed 2019, https://en.wikipedia.org/wiki/ImageNet.

18 Bernard Marr, The Most Amazing Artificial Intelligence Milestones So Far, *Forbes*, 2018, www.forbes.com/sites/bernardmarr/2018/12/31/the-most-amazing-artificial-intelligence-milestones-so-far/#35fe52ef7753.

19 Jo Best, IBM Watson: The Inside Story of How the Jeopardy-Winning Supercomputer Was Born, and What It Wants to Do Next, Tech Republic, 2013, www.techrepublic.com/article/ibm-watson-the-inside-story-of-how-the-jeopardy-winning-supercomputer-was-born-and-what-it-wants-to-do-next/.

20 Venkatraman Krishnan Anirudh,10 Breakthroughs In Artificial Intelligence That Skyrocketed Its Popularity This Decade, Analytics India Magazine, 2019, www.analyticsindiamag.com/10-breakthroughs-in-artificial-intelligence-that-skyrocketed-its-popularity-this-decade/.

21 Anthony Cuthbertson, World champion Go player quits because AI has become too powerful MSN News, 2019, https://www.msn.com/en-gb/news/offbeat/world-champion-go-player-quits-because-ai-has-become-too-powerful/ar-BBXstwt.

22 Allison Linn, Historic Achievement: Microsoft Researchers Reach Human Parity in Conversational Speech Recognition, Microsoft AI Blog, 2016, https://blogs.microsoft.com/ai/historic-achievement-microsoft-researchers-reach-human-parity-conversational-speech-recognition/.

Chapter 5

Do Submarines Swim?

If you were really sick how would you feel about being under the care of a doctor or nurse that is brilliant at the "science" of medicine but unable to explain why they are recommending a treatment, clueless about understanding what you are feeling and not adept at managing the "softer side" of care delivery?

Such is the case with Artificial Intelligence (AI) today.

By taking advantage of the growing array of capabilities defined in Chapter 3, AI holds great promise to improve the quality and effectiveness of health services delivered around the world today. As you set off to plan and execute your organization's AI strategy, a key factor in leveraging its power is to understand what AI is great at and what it's not so good at when it comes to improving things clinicians and consumers care about.

With machine learning, we are able to use massive quantities of data to find patterns that humans simply don't have the ability or time to see. As a result, AI is increasingly good at being able to sense and predict things we care about. This includes things like which patients are at high risk of readmissions, falls, or unexpected deterioration. It can help predict which treatments may produce the best outcomes. It's already making diagnostic images more "intelligent."

Today companies like Microsoft and Google have already created computerized speech and natural language skills that have reached parity with humans. These now power intelligent chatbots capable of automating patient registration, health advisory services, and customer service.

And while these growing capabilities are widening the value proposition of AI in healthcare, there are key areas where it falls short. To further

As "smart" as AI is becoming at certain things, no one has figured out how to have machines be imbued with, or mimic those qualities that are essential to the care process like wisdom, reasoning, judgement, imagination, critical thinking, common sense and empathy.

your understanding of how to delineate what it's good at and what it's not, consider this question: While everyone's talking about Artificial Intelligence, have you ever heard anyone talk about Artificial Wisdom?

As "smart" as AI is becoming at certain things, no one has figured out how to have machines be imbued with, or mimic those qualities that are essential to the care process like wisdom, reasoning, judgment, imagination, critical thinking, common sense, and empathy. Such attributes remain as uniquely human characteristics and essential to the provision of health services.

Managing Different Types of Knowledge

Just prior to his passing in 2018, Paul Allen, the less-recognized cofounder of Microsoft, ponied up $125 million with the Allen Institute for AI to attempt to shed light on whether computers can be "taught" how to have or replicate what we refer to as "common sense." Known as Project Alexandria Allen's goal was to create a database of fundamental knowledge that humans take for granted but machines have always lacked.[1]

Smart machines can recognize certain things that are fact, logic, or pattern based but unable to discern many situations that humans recognize as common sense. For example, through machine learning and a vision application programming interface (API), a computer recognizes objects, but can't explain what it sees. AI can describe how a submarine is propelled through the water but can't differentiate this from swimming. As far as we've come in creating smart devices and computers, they all remain devoid of "common sense" that most humans learn at an early age.

Even the most sophisticated uses of AI today are subject to these limitations. For example, when confronted with heavy traffic or unexpected situations, driverless cars just sit there.

Understanding the differences in the types of knowledge used in health and medicine is key to knowing how to practically apply AI in service of the things we care about. The following story illustrates the types of knowledge that we deal with in the delivery of health services.

In 1945, British philosopher Gilbert Ryle gave a famous lecture about two kinds of knowledge by pointing out that a child knows that a bicycle has two wheels, that its tires are filled with air, and that you ride the bike by pushing its pedals. Ryle termed this kind of knowledge "knowing that." But learning to ride a bicycle involves another type of learning that is acquired by falling off, and by coming to know and experience the effects of gravity as you learn how to balance on two wheels. Ryle termed this experiential, skill-based kind of knowledge "knowing how."

Ryle points out that factual and experiential knowledge are independent. Broadening your factual knowledge does not deepen your experiential knowledge. In other words, "knowing how" cannot be substituted by "knowing that."[2]

In applying the "two types of knowledge" in healthcare, a smart machine can sense or predict temperature variation but doesn't know how a patient feels when they have a fever. Measuring spikes in blood pressure does not equate to understanding what anxiety feels like for a patient or family member and what to do about it.

The dynamics described above are often at the heart of questions and controversies about the role of machines vs. clinicians in the future of healthcare.

One of my favorite books and websites that brings home the value of experience and common sense is from Tyler Vigen called *Spurious Correlations*. Vigen lampoons the treatise that statistical correlations on their own can be used to infer causation.[3]

An example of this issue is noted in the chart in Figure 5.1. Did you know that there is an almost perfect correlation (.95) between the number of people who die by becoming tangled in their bedsheets and the per capita consumption of cheese? Does this mean we can reduce the mortality rate from "death by bedsheets" if we consume less cheese? Probably not.

As you consider how AI will be used to transform health it is critically important to delineate between the hype and reality of its capabilities.

Another great mind in the world today on this topic is Gary Marcus who is a scientist, best-selling author, and researcher of both natural intelligence and AI. Even though he developed and sold a machine learning company to Uber, Marcus is the voice of antihype at a time when AI is all the hype. In a recent interview Marcus brought this subject into focus by musing over the extreme hype surrounding driverless cars: "Google has worked on it

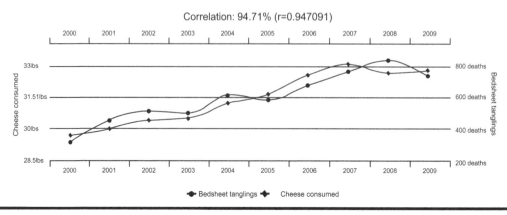

Figure 5.1 Per capita cheese consumption correlates with the number of people who died by becoming tangled in their bedsheets. (*Data*: U. S. Department of Agriculture and Centers for Disease Control & Prevention; *Graph*: Spurious Correlations, Tyler Vigen, tylervigen.com.)

(driverless cars) for 7 years and their car can still only drive on sunny days without too traffic. The average 16-year-old can do this as long as they're sober with a couple of months of training."[4]

Although AI will invariably take on more routine work and augment human decision-making, it will not any time soon provide the experiential knowledge that is critical to the delivery of health services and unique to the humans that provide it. As a result, the application of human experience and expertise to clinician and business decisions and practices will continue to drive how healthcare works for the foreseeable future.

As AI changes the nature of work and employment, innovative leaders will define and execute AI plans that evolve to create performance loops. The result will be scenarios where humans and machines collaborate to get the best from each in pursuit of improving the quality and effectiveness in providing health services.

An example of this is the use of AI to create virtual nursing assistants to automate repetitive activities such as remotely assessing a patient's symptoms and alerting clinicians when patient care is needed. In doing so, AI has the potential to save 20% of a human nurse's time.[5]

The key to creating such a collaboration comes down to understanding the fundamentals of what AI is good at and where its value is human-dependent. In the end, success with AI is about how it is used by clinicians and knowledge workers in helping them achieve their highest levels of performance.

Notes

1 Cade Metz, Paul Allen Wants to Teach Computer Common Sense, *New York Times*, 2018, www.nytimes.com/2018/02/28/technology/paul-allen-ai-common-sense.html.
2 Siddhartha Mukherjee, AI Versus MD – What Happens When Diagnosis is Automated? *New Yorker Magazine*, 2017, www.newyorker.com/magazine/2017/04/03/ai-versus-md.
3 Tyler Vigen, Spurious Correlations, Hachette Books 2015, http://tylervigen.com/spurious-correlations.
4 Gary Marcus, Discussing the Limits of Artificial Intelligence, Tech Crunch, 2017, https://techcrunch.com/2017/04/01/discussing-the-limits-of-artificial-intelligence/?renderMode=ie11.
5 Artificial Intelligence – Healthcare's New Nervous System, Accenture, 2017, www.accenture.com/t20170418T023006__w__/us-en/_acnmedia/PDF 49/Accenture-Health-Artificial-Intelligence.pdf#zoom=50.

Chapter 6

Creating Value Today with AI

AI is a tool. The choice about how it gets deployed is ours.

—Oren Etzioni
CEO, Allen Institute for Artificial Intelligence

Imagine a future when healthcare is able to seamlessly tailor itself to fit the needs of each patient and the clinicians that serve them. It's a world where practitioners and researchers are freed from repetitive administrative tasks. Clinicians are able to leverage all data to better serve patients and consumers. This is a time when Artificial Intelligence (AI)-assisted analytics, simulation, and hypothesis testing help humans drive decision-making strategy and innovation across all care settings.

In the emerging world of intelligent health, AI will increasingly move us towards such customized and on-demand experiences. But we are not there yet.

When it comes to where we are and where we're going with AI in health, I'm reminded of a quote credited to Christopher Columbus: "One does not discover new lands without consenting to lose sight of the shore for a very long time."[1]

As we look forward, the move towards Intelligent Health Systems, will come in stages. We are already seeing the first iterations of where it's making enhancements to existing processes and practices. Over time AI will redefine ways in which we assess, monitor, diagnose, and manage health. What exactly will occur and when it is nearly impossible to predict, but the evolution is definitely underway.

Think for a moment about the evolution of mobile phones. They've been around for a while with the original "transformation" being the ability to talk with others through a device that was untethered to a wire and physical location. Gradually this evolved with technology breakthroughs allowing us to do many other things. We have reached a point where smartphones today seem more like the "device that used to be a phone" as voice calls now represent a small percentage of the time we spend using these devices.

Not dissimilar to the evolution of the smartphone, the AI in health market is in its early stages and is likely to follow the "acceptance and adoption" cycle of other major tech trends that over time became pervasive in use and value within the health industry. For healthcare, the first phase of any major tech adoption cycle typically occurs over the course of a decade.

Beyond the historical adoption cycle we've seen with other new technologies, AI is different in that next-generation health and medical systems using AI will benefit from the continuous learning nature of it. Just as humans do, health and medical AI systems will learn and adjust from past experiences based on patient and doctor responses and the outcomes seen from these systems over time. For example, decision support systems of the future will look completely unrecognizable next to today's systems that are mainly based on fixed, rules-based programming. Future systems will likely move towards assimilating all accumulated data with diagnostic systems being automated with a dynamic set of algorithms.

With this in mind, your AI strategy should be bookended with a broad vision for change on one side, and a clear and pragmatic view of where the AI in health market is today. This includes deciding the areas in which you initially invest your time, attention, and resources. Let's look at what's happening now in the practical adoption and use of AI today and in the near term. We'll look ahead to more futuristic use cases that build on today's efforts in Chapter 15.

Today's High Value Use Cases

While the future is bright for AI, health leaders see many immediate opportunities for its use to drive measurable value. In a survey of health provider and payer executives, the Society of Actuaries found that 57% of executives believe predictive analytics will save their organization 15% or more over the next 5 years, with 26% forecasting saving 25% or more over the next 5 years.[2] As noted in the chart below, the most valuable outcomes expected from

	PROVIDERS	PAYERS
Patient Satisfaction	53%	35%
Cost	36%	51%
Profitability	37%	47%
Clinical outcomes	41%	37%
Staffing/workforce needs	46%	29%
Hospital readmissions	48%	23%
Patient demand/population shifts	38%	31%
Reimbursement	34%	26%
Disease/illness risk	28%	32%
Diagnosis	34%	20%
Identify waste	27%	25%
Adverse events	29%	20%
Mortality	24%	24%
Inventory needs	25%	21%
ID fraud/misrepresentation	17%	28%

Figure 6.1 Most valuable use of predictive analytics – providers versus payers. (Society of Actuaries.)

AI vary among providers and payers. Patient satisfaction was selected most among providers, while cost was selected most among payers (Figure 6.1).

AI applications with a proven return on investment (ROI) are gaining prominence in the current market across clinical and nonclinical use cases. Examples include workflow and resource optimization, elimination of unnecessary procedures and costs, and clinical and business decision support.

Clinical Opportunities

There is an abundance of AI use-case opportunities in the clinical realm being pursued today. In reviewing the current and near-term uses and investments being made globally, the analysts at Frost and Sullivan see a set of scenarios unfolding over the next few years in keeping with market needs and readiness as noted in Figure 6.2.[3]

Clinical decision support (CDS) is an area seeing rapid growth as the application of AI and machine learning serves to automate the processes of evidence-based clinical and scientific decision-making. General areas where this is being used include population health management, precision medicine, and predictive analytics at the Point of Care (PoC).

Chronic condition management is an area where AI can assist clinicians in providing better intuitive care management for chronic patients. AI solutions can be used to transform the status quo, which is characterized by data noninteroperability, provider burnout, and care leakages. Integration

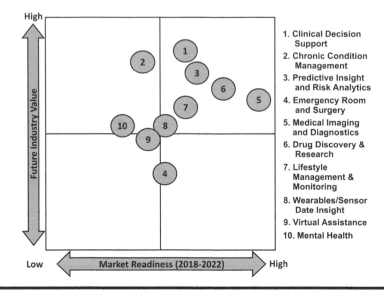

Figure 6.2   Top 10 AI applications in healthcare: opportunity assessment framework, global, 2018–2022. (Frost and Sullivan 2019.)

of lifestyle data with AI platforms can provide compelling near-term benefits for preventive care practice. General areas of focus include population health risk stratification, predictive analytics for preventive care as well as guidance for optimal disease management.

Predictive insights and risk analytics are being provided through AI-powered tools that manage clinical risks and are seeing a strong uptake in the market. Current areas of focus include predicting and reducing medical errors, preventable inpatient readmissions, hospital-acquired infections, and adverse drug reactions.

PREDICTIVE CARE GUIDANCE: PREVENTING CARDIAC ARRESTS WITH AI

In the future AI may make television shows about doctors and hospitals much less interesting. In almost every episode we see doctors and nurses racing down the halls, white lab coats flapping, as they rush to "save" a patient that had just been "coded" because their heart had stopped unexpectantly. But what if doctors could see into the future and know who is about to code, so they could prevent a code from happening in the first place? The use of AI at Ochsner Health System (Ochsner) is doing just that.

Clinicians at this U.S.-based health system are making use of a cloud-based machine learning platform that serves as an intelligent "triage" tool.

The system analyzes thousands of data points in near real time to predict which patients will deteriorate in the near future. It then triggers "precode" alerts that help care teams proactively assess and intervene with patients who are at high risk.

Predictive models used to drive such use cases require massive amounts of data. Ochsner Health took advantage of its unified data infrastructure made possible by its EHR vendor. This allowed the health system to effectively query a large data set from 11 hospitals. Their previous focus on modernizing their data estate enabled Ochsner to build, train, and validate a model to predict patient deterioration.

Beyond building the data model and applying machine learning in a real care setting, Ochsner's leadership focused its efforts on engaging clinicians to help ensure that its efforts to integrate the system with the "human workflow" were successful. This included involving clinicians in things like fine-tuning the timing and frequency of alerts. Too few alerts might miss high-risk patients, but too many would produce alert fatigue. Alerts sent too soon didn't convey urgency, while those sent too late didn't allow for interventions. A four-hour warning turned out to be ideal, giving enough time for a rapid response provider to finish what she's doing, walk – not run – to a patient's room and conduct an evaluation. Interventions may be a medication change, transfer to ICU or another form of elevated care.

A key factor in the success of Ochsner's efforts is in how it reinforced that such tools are designed to augment rather than supplant the expertise and wisdom of a clinician. In this case the value of AI is providing predictive guidance by leveraging the value of the systems data to help busy clinicians better manage the care of their patients.

In the initial pilot of the system, Ochsner successfully reduced the hospital's typical number of codes by 44%. It's now expanding the technology to a twenty-four-hour schedule and to more hospitals in its network.[31]

Emergency departments are increasingly benefiting from predictive tools that forecast the flow of patients. These are finding immediate application for better management of human and material resources in areas where there are high patient volumes and variance in demand for services. Areas of focus include predicting patient flow and utilization and improved ability to forecast staffing, expenses, and revenue.

Medical imaging and diagnostics are making use of AI solutions by enabling radiologists to interpret hidden disease patterns from clinical images and drive more personalized diagnosis at a greater speed and scale. Areas of focus include general imaging, cardiovascular, breast imaging, and image-guided therapies.

AI-assisted surgery is improving surgical outcomes by helping surgeons perform better and reducing surgeon variation. While robotic -assisted surgeries have been around for some time, this next generation of surgical robotics helps surgeons to determine what is happening during complex surgical procedures by providing real-time data points about the movements the surgeon makes during the procedure. Additionally, AI is being used to provide real-time predictions that assist anesthesiologists during surgery to improve compliance and machine learning for modeling surgical workflow.

Drug discovery & research is a costly and time-consuming process where AI technologies are being applied to reduce inefficiencies across the full research and development lifecycle. Currently the majority of AI projects in this area focus on the early discovery or preclinical research phases, with natural language processing (NLP) being employed during the early phases of research. Areas of focus include target-based and phenotypic drug discovery, analyzing biomedical, clinical, and patient data and analyzing research literature, publications, and patents.

Clinical trials and patient recruitment are getting a lift from AI as it provides for the ability to sort through greater volumes of data in a shorter period of time to find patterns that increase the likelihood of finding the right candidates for clinical trials and research.

Improving the use and effectiveness of Electronic Health Records (EHRs) is an area where AI can come to the rescue in improving usability. Many EHRs are built on older underlying technologies that are complex and difficult to navigate. As a result, clinicians often struggle with matching the use of EHRs with how they actually practice.

Promising options in the use of AI to make existing EHR systems more flexible and intelligent include the use of intelligent text mining to improve data extraction from free text such as provider notes, use of diagnostic or predictive algorithms to warn clinicians of high-risk conditions such as sepsis. Other uses include automating clinical documentation and data entry with the use of NLP, capturing clinical notes with NLP and smart clinical decision support (CDS) which moves systems away from traditional rule-based system and towards the use of machine learning that provides more dynamic and personalized decision support capabilities.[4]

NORTHWEST MEDICAL SPECIALTIES IMPROVING THE QUALITY OF CARE FOR CANCER PATIENTS WITH AI

Northwest Medical Specialties (NWMS) is a leading oncology practice in the Seattle, Washington area. At any given time, their team of cancer specialists is actively managing the needs of 10,000 patients.

When it comes to providing quality care, there are many variables to be assessed and managed, which determine both outcomes and quality of life for cancer patients. Beyond deciding on the best treatment options and modalities, the quality of care and the patient experience is determined by other areas such as pain management, depression, functional deterioration, and mortality risks. For those patients dealing with end-of-life care such variables are critically important and can be both challenging and rewarding for patients and providers when done well.

The clinical leadership of NWMS decided to make use of predictive analytics within their practice with an initial focus on using it to proactively assess patients in active treatment for their risks relating to depression and pain management.

Using near-real-time data feeds, NWMS utilized a form of machine learning to assess and risk-rate patients for specific variables like signs of depression as they went through the treatment process. This continuous assessment using AI allows them to essentially rate and understand where each patient is on a measurable scale for variables critical to understanding and managing things like depression and pain in real time, or in some cases, before it happens. The initial use of AI to proactively risk rate and predict patients produced the following outcomes:

Depression is screened for regularly and in spite of that, it often remains an underdiagnosed and untreated problem. In a 6-month time period, NWMS utilized real-time and predictive assessments resulting in identifying heightened depression risk in approximately 10% of their patients. The increased use of automated screening and subsequent treatment resulted in a 13% reduction in patients with active depression as a diagnosis.

Pain management is another significant challenge in this population, and in the same 6-month time frame there was a dramatic improvement in pain management. By the sixth month, an average of 185 fewer patients per month were registering severe pain scores (compared to baseline), and overall there was a 33% reduction in patients reporting moderate and severe pain.

As disease progression occurs, functional decline is a major concern. While in many cases decline is unavoidable, there is a subset of patients where such decline can be predicted and prevented with targeted interventions. NWMS applied the same intelligent assessment process to identify and prevent functional decline in their patient population. Over a short period of time, the monthly rate of patients with a documented functional declined by 18%.

Bolstering Patient Engagement and Satisfaction

The ultimate goal of Intelligent Health Systems is to provide an efficient, personalized experience for each patient and consumer. While fulfilling this vision at scale may be something that happens in the future, there are a number of use cases being successfully deployed now to provide more intelligent and convenient consumer experiences.

Lifestyle management & monitoring is an area benefiting from AI-powered analytics. When applied to the increasing burden of lifestyle-driven chronic health conditions, AI-powered platforms can help patients and their families make healthier decisions. AI also provides compelling applications across health reward and motivation platforms to achieve the desired health and wellness goals. From remote monitoring, smartphone apps, and wearable devices, areas of focus include chronic disease monitoring, treatment adherence, and preventive care programs.

Personalized responses to consumers are now possible with the use of Conversational AI. Chatbots are AI-based conversation agents being used in a variety of consumer-engagement scenarios to simulate human interactions and provide immediate, personalized responses. Conversational AI goes beyond traditional automated response systems to provide cognitive responses that mimic humans that can eliminate frustrating delays and errors in customer service, particularly for handling customer complaints.

The application of conversational AI allows for more efficient and regular communication between patients and care providers to support administrative tasks including referrals, patient satisfaction surveys, appointment scheduling, billing, and insurance verification.

CINCINNATI CHILDREN'S HOSPITAL CREATES DIGITAL CONCIERGE WITH MOBILE APP AND CHATBOT

Cincinnati Children's Hospital Medical Center is well known for the excellence of its care and its commitment to the well-being of the families it serves. To reduce strain for parents and make their lives easier, the hospital created the Caren mobile app and chatbot to help parents get answers to questions and to help them entertain their children.

The goal of creating Caren was to essentially provide a digital concierge. Through Caren, families can easily find their way through the medical center, look up locations and wait times at urgent care centers, and get real-time updates of their child's surgery status. Caren can also give them a digital parking pass and let them store their parking location for later reference. For questions that aren't already included in the app, Caren provides a natural language chatbot for answers, along with jokes and a scavenger hunt throughout the hospital.[30]

Predicting and preventing customer experience issues from occurring is made possible through the power of AI to parse through large bodies of data to spot patterns that otherwise might not be seen. The use of AI-enabled analytics as part of the customer journey analytics can find every single relationship in the data that exists—*without expressly being told to look for it.* It can predict the likelihood of future behaviors with high accuracy and find the inhibitors of current customer performance.

Personalizing consumer engagement activities, whether for an individual or a broad population, is enabled by AI and becoming a vital service for both providers and insurance companies looking to build loyalty, promote wellness, and reduce long-term spending. The application of smart analytics tools to create consumer profiles allow health organizations to provide tailored messaging, improve customer retention, and keep patients engaged with their financial and clinical responsibilities.

PREVENTING BLINDNESS WITH COMPUTER VISION AND MACHINE LEARNING

Diabetes is the leading cause of preventable blindness in working aged adults in the United States and other countries, but up until the use of AI, there was no easy way for primary care providers (PCPs) to independently diagnose diabetic vision damage. That's why retinal surgeon Dr. Sunil Gupta created an AI platform that identifies diabetic retinopathy, often before patients realize they suffer from vision loss.

It is estimated that **415 million** people are living with diabetes in the world today, which is estimated to be 1 in 11 of the world's adult population. This figure is expected to rise to **642 million** people living with diabetes worldwide by 2040.[27] Diabetic retinopathy is found in almost 40% of all people with diabetes and in nearly all people who have had diabetes for 20 years or more. It is more frequent in those of African and Latino ancestry.

Diabetic retinopathy is an eye condition that affects the retinas of people with diabetes. It is caused by changes in the blood vessels of the eye as a result of high blood sugar (glucose). The person's sight is often not affected until the condition is severe. A patient can have 20/20 vision and still be on the verge of losing their eyesight. And while the risk of diabetic retinopathy can be identified with a simple evaluation, most PCPs traditionally do not perform this noninvasive exam during a clinic visit. Historically, a yearly visit to an ophthalmologist or optometrist was recommended for a diabetic retinopathy exam. This situation led to as many as half of the people with diabetes not getting the annual eye exams, and they need to diagnose this disease in its early stages.

To address these challenges and reduce the number of people who suffer from vision loss and blindness from diabetes, Dr. Gupta developed Intelligent Retinal Imaging Systems (IRIS), a fully integrated system that utilizes a simple, high-quality camera to capture the image of the retina in the back of the eye and then makes use of machine learning to identify diabetic retinopathy and determine if a patient is at risk of vision loss. The cloud-based system makes it easy for a minimally trained staff member in a primary care clinic to take an image of the retina, which can then be rapidly evaluated using a deep learning (algorithm. Once the process is complete, the system triggers an alert to a clinician that the results are available for review.

IRIS is a system that empowers health systems to innovate the way in which services can be rendered resulting in increased compliance with diabetic management protocols and improved outcomes. An example of how AI can drive innovation across a population can be found in West Virginia.

As a rural state West Virginia has special challenges when it comes to eye care for diabetics. Sixty-four percent of West Virginians with diabetes are at risk for blindness. Due to many barriers like transportation, education, and economics, many do not seek out preventive care including an annual Diabetic Eye Evaluation.

It was against this backdrop that West Virginia University Medicine teamed up with the West Virginia Practice-Based Research Network (a partnership of primary care clinicians and research entities that work to address community-based health issues) to look at how AI might be used to close the care gap. Together they initially implemented IRIS at three primary care sites across the state and two Western Virginia University sites.[28] In the first 13 months of the program the collaboration performed over 1,500 exams. The initial program focused on recruiting diabetic patients that had a known gap for an annual diabetic eye exam. The results during this time demonstrated that the AI-enabled process was making a difference in closing the care gap including:

- 31% of patients examined had an identifiable pathology
- 16% of patients were diagnosed with diabetic retinopathy and would otherwise have potentially gone undiagnosed and untreated
- More than 24% of patients being examined were identified and referred for diabetic retinopathy and other ocular pathologies such as glaucoma, cataracts, or macular degeneration.[29]

Beyond these numbers, the pilot improved quality care measures including improved compliance with patients receiving annual eye exams.

With the number of people with diabetic retinopathy was expected to double by 2050 AI will play a crucial role in helping clinicians improve the management of this and other chronic conditions.

Operational and Financial Opportunities

The use of AI and machine learning to improve financial, revenue cycle, and operational performance is seeing a lot of uptake as the "time to value" can be shorter than clinical use cases, returns are more easily measured, and, in some use cases, there is less complexity in the data requirements needed to complete and launch projects.

AI-driven operational command centers leverage massive amounts of information generated by health organizations to find and fix operational inefficiencies in real time. AI command centers equipped with predictive tools pull together data from multiple IT systems to help prioritize activity in specific sections of the hospital based on need. This allows the hospital to assign beds faster, discharge patients more quickly, and accept more complex and time-consuming cases.

Operations-focused AI is also helping improve efficiencies by optimizing scheduling for clinical departments with a high volume of procedures such as Surgery, Cath, and GI labs. By predicting how much time each procedure will take, these AI-driven scheduling solutions reduce the amount of time high-volume procedure rooms go empty, in addition to reducing wait times and maximizing the use of operating rooms and lab facilities.

Reducing appointment no-shows and cancellations is occurring due to the use of predictive analytics to identify which patients are likely to skip an appointment without advance notice. Using past patient data, patient demographics, location, and environmental factors, algorithms can predict who will show up late, who will cancel, and who will be no-show. The average cost of a no-show is $200 per patient.[5] AI gives providers the chance to send additional reminders and offer transportation or other services to increase the chance of patients making appointments.

Optimizing patient throughput in clinic and hospital settings is being done by monitoring a host of factors in near real time with predictive capabilities to proactively signal when volumes, space, and staffing are out of synch.

Optimizing staffing is being done with the help of AI with a specialized focus on predicting and better managing resource matching to address fluctuations based on future patient volumes, flow, and acuity. Using AI to predict patterns in utilization helps to not only ensure optimal staffing levels but also contribute to reduced wait times and improved patient satisfaction.

Augmenting staff with the use of virtual nursing assistants could reduce unnecessary hospital visits and lessen the burden on medical professionals. In one study 64% of patients reported they would be comfortable with AI virtual nurse assistants, citing the benefits of 24/7 access to answers and support, round-the-clock monitoring, and the ability to get quick answers to questions about medications.[6]

Improving supply chain management through the use of AI represents one of the most significant opportunities for health organizations today to improve cost efficiencies and trim unnecessary spending. AI assists supply chain management specialists by assessing and spotting variation patterns and by providing more actionable insights into ordering patterns and supply utilization.

Strengthening IT security by helping security systems identify critical issues using human behavior and analytics. Today, you're more likely to experience a data breach of at least 10,000 records than you are to catch the flu this winter.[7] The cost of a data breach per compromised record is now $148, with organizations taking an average of 196 days to detect a breach.[8] AI-enhanced security uses machine learning, analytics, and orchestration to help human responders identify and contain breaches with good results, saving an average of $8 per compromised record.[9]

Billing errors and denials are seeing a lot of uptake in the use of AI. According to research from the American Medical Association, the health industry could save $15.5 billion each year if claims were processed correctly the first time.[10] Such errors drive up costs and slow down revenue. Health organizations today are applying machine learning to prospectively rate and predict which claims are at risk of being denied and then proactively resolving issues which automatically expedite claims and payments.

Prior authorization is being improved with the use of computer vision and machine learning in combination to automate the highly repetitive nature of the prior authorization process.

Clinical quality improvement initiatives are providing strong financial returns as AI is used to improve quality and reduce variance in care delivery processes. Use cases such as predicting and preventing readmissions, hospital-acquired infections, and falls provide a secondary benefit of reducing resource utilization and lengths of stay (LOS), thereby improving the financial returns of health organizations operating in fixed pay or at-risk reimbursement environments.

Fraud detection and prevention is an expensive problem for healthcare organizations and also for insurers. Fraud detection has traditionally relied on a combination of computerized (rules-based) and manual reviews of medical claims. It's a time-consuming process that hinges on being able to quickly spot anomalies after the incident occurs in order to intervene. Health insurers are experimenting with AI-supported data mining, coupled with AI-based neural networks (which mimic the processes of the human brain, but much more quickly) to search Medicare claims for patterns associated with medical reimbursement fraud.

Today, more than 75% of insurers report the use of machine learning algorithms to flag fraud cases.[11]

CUTTING LABOR & CARE COSTS BY PREDICTING & REDUCING LENGTH OF STAY (LOS)

Headquartered in Boston, Massachusetts, Steward Health Care is a leading accountable care organization with 1.5 million covered lives that are managed through the company's managed care and health insurance services. It also operates 38 hospitals in Malta and the United States and has about 40,000 clinicians and employees.

And with 1.5 million covered lives for which the organization is at full risk for managing services, Steward Health has a relentless focus on leveraging technology to improve both the quality and efficiency of delivering care. To this end Steward Health Care effectively leveraged AI in their quest to address this question: "What if we could predict the length of stay (LOS) at the time of admission so that we'd immediately know more precisely how to staff and which patients would need tighter coordination and scheduling to reduce their LOS?

There is often a wide variance in the average lengths of stay (ALOS) for hospitals within a region or nation with as many as 20% of these hospital days being avoidable. Research conducted in various countries shows that a substantial proportion of hospital days are not needed or wasted. Beyond the waste of economic and human resources, research also shows that prolonged hospital stays can be detrimental to patients as they are exposed to a variety of risks such as hospital-acquired infections and other adverse events.[25] The challenge in managing LOS is often a matter of judgment to ensure an appropriate LOS. For example, in the last decade many health systems that have focused on reducing their readmissions rates have seen their ALOS rise because getting the risk scores down for patients with the greatest readmission risk requires longer LOSs.

In keeping with its focus on using data and predictive capabilities to improve performance, Steward Health Care engaged in a project to develop a system using AI and machine learning that would allow them to risk rate each patient and predict a LOS. To accomplish this, the organization built a predictive model using a 4-year regression analysis of every patient admitted. In addition, the system utilizes multiple other external data types such as flu, seasonality, and social data to assist in accurately predicting future patient volumes.

The results of this work now allow Steward Health Care to predict inpatient volumes one to two weeks out with 98% accuracy. By providing greater insights into the care path for each patient the system has also reduced the average LOS for patients by one and a half days. Steward Health Care estimates that the ability to predict and better manage LOS is saving $48 million per year. Additional benefits that have been seen include improved nurse scheduling and a higher level of patient satisfaction.[26]

Opportunities for Intelligent Health Payers

While many of the articles written on the benefit of AI in health focus on the provider side of health and medical services, there are a myriad of opportunities to help solve for many of the administrative and cost challenges of health payers today. According to a study by Accenture, insurers could save up to $7 billion over 18 months using AI-driven technologies by streamlining administrative processes.[12] By automating routine business tasks alone, the study projects that health insurers could save $15 million per 100 full-time employees. In response, three-fourths of health insurance executives (72%) say investing in AI is one of their top strategic priorities.[13]

With eight out of every ten claims being potentially incorrect or fraudulent, up to 80% of all claims must be reviewed by a human adjuster. AI is transforming claims processing with the use of algorithms to automatically flag discrepancies to save time and money.[14]

Automating customer service is another area where AI is coming to the rescue. Today, 68% of insurers are already using chatbots in various segments of their business. One estimate is that health insurance companies could save more than $2 billion annually by using AI to manage customer interactions.[15] An example of chatbots becoming pervasive in the insurance industry is ZhongAn Tech, China's largest insurance company. From applying for coverage and checking benefits to filing a medical claim, 97% of all consumer interactions are done through a chatbot with only the most complex inquiries being handled by a human representative.[16]

Health payers large and small are leaning into the use of AI to transform the way business is done. Cigna, for example, is tapping into AI to solve some of healthcare's most crucial problems and to further advance personal health for its customers and clients while lowering actuarial risks. Cigna Ventures, Cigna's corporate venture fund is actively focused on identifying and investing in early-stage innovative companies in three core areas that include insights and analytics, digital health, and care delivery.[17]

Opportunities for Intelligent Pharma and Drug Discovery

Every year a few dozen drugs make their way into the market after going through a rigorous development and approval process. For every one that makes it to market several thousand other drug candidates fall by the wayside. Just one of every ten therapies that enter human clinical trials makes it to the pharmacy.[18] On average the research and development journey for each drug that actually comes to market take 12 years at an average cost of $2.6 billion.[19]

Discovering and bringing new drugs to market is notoriously slow and costly for a reason. Science moves slowly because of the incredibly complex nature of human biology. It's been almost two decades since the human genome was sequenced. Since that time researchers have found treatments for a small fraction of the 7,000 known rare diseases. These numbers are further complicated as there are approximately 20,000 genes that can malfunction in at least 100,000 ways, making it virtually impossible for drug researchers to probe all of those combinations by hand or with the traditional technologies that have been at their disposal.[20]

It is against this background that drug researchers and developers are turning to machine learning and other AI technologies to make the hunt for new pharmaceuticals quicker, cheaper, and more effective.

While drug research and development processes have made use of machine learning for some time an area holding great promise is the use of Deep Learning (DL). This is a class of machine learning that uses artificial neural networks (ANNs) that are applied to innovate areas such as compound property and activity prediction, chemoinformatics (generation of new chemical structures), predicting reactions, retrosynthetic analysis, and biological imaging analysis.[21]

AI is also streamlining the traditional process used by the industry in selecting patients for clinical trials and enable pharma companies to identify any issues with compounds much earlier when it comes to efficacy and safety (Figure 6.3).

Matching AI to Clinical and Business Needs

As noted by the use cases above, there is no shortage of how AI is being applied today to drive measurable value in quality, outcomes, efficiencies, and the consumer experience.

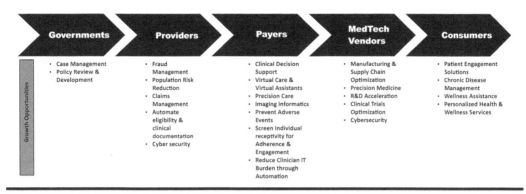

**Figure 6.3   Current and near-term opportunities for AI in health (through 2025).
(Frost and Sullivan 2019.)**

A key to success is creating a plan that defines the most valuable starting points for your initial investments in AI, which are then executed in a coordinated fashion in keeping with your goals and measures of success.

In most health organizations, early use cases start within a department or clinical division where strong interest exists among clinicians or staff with an early adopter mindset. As such projects come forward, the chances for success increase when they become part of an organizational framework by which all projects are sanctioned and supported. This framework should include defining the complexity of each project, the availability of data and expertise needed to complete and deploy projects, timeline, metrics, and whether a project is treated as pilot or is seen as eventually moving into full production.

Barriers to Adoption

While there are many powerful use cases producing value today, challenges remain in the enterprise-wide adoption and use of AI by health organizations.

As a central theme to this book, the successful adoption of AI requires an alignment between people, processes, and technology. From a tactical perspective, building and ensuring trust, upskilling talent, having a clearly defined AI strategy, along with ways to measure ROI are among the top challenges that hinder successful AI adoption.

A survey of the current thinking by health system executives indicates that the most common challenge in their AI journey is defining the right use cases and the need for clarity in measuring the Return on Investment (ROI).

Here are some of the most common barriers to mobilizing an effective plan to harness the power of AI in health organizations today:

AI Won't Live up to Expectations: Like other technology promises that came before, AI is often overhyped with a certain degree of skepticism among health leaders and decision-makers. While a recent survey of health executives by Intel shows the majority expect widespread adoption of AI in health in the next 5 years, over half are also skeptical or concerned about the impact of implementing AI today. The findings showed that 54% believe AI will be responsible for a fatal error, 53% said AI will be poorly implemented or won't work properly, with 49% believing that AI has been overhyped and not likely to meet expectations.[22]

Given the hype surrounding AI in health, a certain degree of resistance is to be expected. When it comes to successfully adopting AI, the best counterbalance to skepticism is to collaborate across functions to create a robust vision upfront. This can then be tied to practical starting points including initial use cases, how you will use AI to differentiate your organization from competitors, and how you'll measure ROI.

Lack of Executive Support: Beyond the skepticism noted above some clinical and business leaders often don't understand AI technology or how it can be useful. As a result, they fail to champion AI initiatives and can also be known to sabotage planning and investments. A survey by IDC found that 49% of enterprises deploying AI technology experienced challenges with stakeholder buy-in.[23]

Employee Resistance and Job Security: In a survey of 1,000 managers, 42% believe AI will eliminate jobs and 40% believe that employees lack the skills needed for AI adoption. Overcoming employee resistance is a critical factor in the success of any AI initiatives. Chapter 7 (When AI Meets HR) provides details as to the issues and recommendations for fostering an AI-ready culture to augment your staff with innovation.

Lack of Data and Expertise: With the increasing demand for AI adoption across all industries and limited talent pool, healthcare organizations are finding it difficult to initiate AI-based projects due to the lack of resources. At the same time there is an almost overwhelming set of needs to build and support a data estate foundation for data preparation, exploration, and use. The degree of difficulty is often compounded by issues such as data availability and quality.

The development of a clear IT and data staffing plan which supports the creation and management of your organization's data estate will help to overcome these issues (See Chapter 11).

Lack of Interoperability: Interoperability plays a significant role in supporting data sharing, which is at the heart of what powers almost all AI applications. Without access to comprehensive data from various sources, AI will not be able to offer its full benefits to healthcare.

AI Budget Availability: In a survey of health leaders by the Society of Actuaries, the lack of funding for AI initiatives was cited as the biggest challenge to implementation within their organization even though the majority or leaders surveyed believed AI would provide measurable financial benefit within 5 years.[24]

Lack of Cloud Adoption: While AI can be done with on premise solutions, much of its power and usefulness comes from having data and applications in the cloud. Unfortunately, some healthcare organizations are still hesitant to move data to the cloud. This results in some organizations abandoning the use of cloud-based AI applications in healthcare and resorting to on-premises solutions that may have limited capabilities and potentially more complexity due to the IT environment requirements. Details on the role of the cloud in AI are provided in Chapter 10.

When it comes to understanding and managing transformational change brought about by technology, Microsoft's founder Bill Gates has a lot of history to go on. In this regard his view is worth considering when it comes to finding the balance between the broad vision for AI and making things real and impactful today: "We always overestimate the change that will occur in the next 2 years and underestimate the change that will occur in the next ten."

A bold vision for your organization's intelligent future that's backed by a solid plan for getting started is the focus of this book.

Notes

1 AZ Quotes, www.azquotes.com/quote/1096733.
2 2017 Predictive Analytics in Healthcare Trend Forecast, Society of Actuaries, 2018, www.soa.org/globalassets/assets/Files/programs/predictive-analytics/2017-health-care-trend.pdf.
3 Artificial Intelligence—Top 10 Applications in Healthcare, Global, 2018–2022, Frost and Sullivan, 2019.
4 Thomas Hayes Davenport, Tonya M. Hongsermeier, Kimberly Alba Mc Cord, Using AI to Improve Electronic Health Records, *Harvard Business Review*, 2018, https://hbr.org/2018/12/using-ai-to-improve-electronic-health-records.

5 Parviz Kheirkhah, Qianmei Feng, Lauren M. Travis, Shahriar Tavakoli-Tabasi, Amir Sharafkhaneh, Prevalence, Predictors and Economic Consequences of No-Shows, US National Library of Medicine National Institutes of Health, 2016, www.ncbi.nlm.nih.gov/pmc/articles/PMC4714455/.

6 Deena Zaidi, The 3 Most Valuable Applications of AI in Health Care, VentureBeat, 2018, https://venturebeat.com/2018/04/22/the-3-most-valuable-applications-of-ai-in-health-care/.

7 Larry Ponman, Calculating the Cost of a Data Breach in 2018, the Age of AI and the IoT, Security Intelligence, 2018, https://securityintelligence.com/ponemon-cost-of-a-data-breach-2018/.

8 Ibid.

9 Ibid.

10 Andrew Stern, US Doctors Say 1 in 5 Insurance Claims Mishandled, Reuters, 2010, www.reuters.com/article/doctors-insurers/corrected-us-doctors-say-1-in-5-insurance-claims-mishandled-idUSN1422071220100615.

11 The State of Insurance Fraud Technology, Coalition Against Insurance Fraud, 2016, www.insurancefraud.org/downloads/State_of_Insurance_Fraud_Technology2016.pdf.

12 Technology Vision for Insurance, Accenture, 2017, www.accenture.com/us-en/insight-insurance-technology-vision-2017.

13 Ibid.

14 Steffen Hehner, Boris Körs, Artificial Intelligence in Health Insurance: Smart Claims Management with Self-Learning Software. McKensey & Company, 2017, www.mckinsey.com/industries/healthcare-systems-and-services/our-insights/artificial-intelligence-in-health-insurance-smart-claims-management-with-self-learning-software.

15 Technology Vision for Insurance, Accenture, 2017, www.accenture.com/us-en/insight-insurance-technology-vision-2017.

16 Karen Yeung, Online Insurer Zhong an Uses Artificial Intelligence to Improve Its Products, South China Morning Post, 2017, www.scmp.com/business/investor-relations/stock-quote-profile/article/2117527/online-insurer-zhongan-uses.

17 Tracey Walker, Cigna Leverages AI, Managed Healthcare Executive, 2019, www.managedhealthcareexecutive.com/technology/cigna-leverages-ai.

18 Robert Langreth, AI Drug Hunters Could Give Big Pharma a Run for Its Money, Bloomberg, 2019, www.bloomberg.com/news/features/2019-07-15/google-ai-could-challenge-big-pharma-in-drug-discovery.

19 Ingrid Torjesen, Drug Development: The journey of a medicine from lab to shelf, *The Pharmacy Journal*, www.pharmaceutical-journal.com/publications/tomorrows-pharmacist/drug-development-the-journey-of-a-medicine-from-lab-to-shelf/20068196.article?firstPass=false.

20 Ibid.

21 Hongming Chen, Ola Engkvist, Yinhai Wang, Marcus Olivecrona, Thomas Blaschke, The Rise of Deep Learning in Drug Discovery, *Drug Discovery Today*, 2018, www.sciencedirect.com/science/article/pii/ S1359644617303598#bib0305.

22 Rajiv Leventhal, Survey of AI Reveals Adoption Predictions, Fears, Healthcare Innovation, 2018, www.hcinnovationgroup.com/population-health-management/ news/13030499/survey-of-ai-reveals-adoption-predictions-fears.

23 Staying Ahead of the Game with Artificial Intelligence, IDC, 2018, https://blog. datarobot.com/infographic-staying-ahead-game-artificial-intelligence.

24 2017 Predictive Analytics in Healthcare Trend Forecast, Society of Actuaries, 2017, www.soa.org/globalassets/assets/Files/programs/predictive-analytics/2017-health-care-trend.pdf.

25 Caterina Caminiti, Tiziana Meschi, Luca Braglia, Francesca Diodati, Elisa Iezzi, Barbara Marcomini, Antonio Nouvenne, Eliana Palermo, Beatrice Prati, Tania Schianchi, Loris Borghi, Reducing unnecessary hospital days to improve quality of care through physician accountability: A cluster randomised trial, *BMC Health Services Research*, 2013, www.ncbi.nlm.nih.gov/pmc/articles/ PMC3577481/.

26 Clifford Goldsmith MD, Three Ways Analytics Are Improving Clinical Outcomes, *Microsoft Industry Blogs*, 2019, https://cloudblogs.microsoft.com/industry-blog/ health/2019/03/13/three-ways-analytics-are-improving-clinical-outcomes/.

27 Diabetes Prevalence, Diabetes.co.uk, accessed 2019, www.diabetes.co.uk/ diabetes-prevalence.html.

28 West Virginia University Case Study, IRIS Website, accessed 2019, https:// retinalscreenings.com/customers/case-studies/west-virginia-university.

29 Ibid.

30 Cincinnati Children's Makes Tough Times Easier with Family-Friendly Mobile App, Microsoft Customer Story, 2018, https://customers.microsoft.com/en-us/ story/cincinnati-childrens-hospital-health-provider-azure.

31 Vanessa Ho, Ochsner Health System: Preventing Cardiac Arrests with AI That Predicts Which Patients Will 'Code', *Microsoft Blog*, 2018, https://news. microsoft.com/transform/ochsner-ai-prevents-cardiac-arrests-predicts-codes/.

Chapter 7

The Leadership Imperative

I don't want to fight old battles. I want to fight new ones.

—Satya Nadella
CEO, Microsoft

When it comes to the disruptive nature of Artificial Intelligence (AI) and the transition to Intelligent Health Systems, there's a lesson to be learned in a pair of photographs found on the next page that were taken in New York City in the early part of the last century. The images are of the Flatiron Building viewed from across the intersection of Broadway, Fifth Avenue, and East 23rd Street, and they are strikingly similar except for one important feature.

In Figure 7.1, taken in 1905, the primary mode of transportation is equine – horses haul carts laden with freight, horse-drawn carriages convey people, and horse-drawn cabs sit curbside waiting for fares.

In Figure 7.2, taken 20 years later, not a single horse can be seen. Instead, a long line of automobiles snakes down Broadway, parked cars jam the curbs, and a stretch of pavement in front of the Flatiron Building has been converted to a parking lot.

What happened in between was a period of profound transformation and disruption. In 1905, it took more than 100,000 horses to move goods and people through New York City. Tens of thousands of people were employed feeding and cleaning up after them. Thousands more worked as blacksmiths, wheelwrights, saddlemakers, and carriage builders. Nationwide, one-quarter of the country's agricultural output was dedicated to growing crops to feed horses.

Two decades later, a new form of horsepower predominated. The result fueled innovation that gave rise to new industries, generated vast numbers

Figure 7.1   Flatiron Builiding circa 1905.

Figure 7.2   Flatiron Building circa 1925.

of new jobs, and transformed the economy. But it was also a 20-year span that saw the end of a generation-old way of life and the dawn of a new kind of society – not just in New York but in cities around the world. During that time, entire categories of work that had provided a good living for people for centuries all but disappeared. Entirely new ways of working and living emerged that carried use forward for decades. The realities of a society that suddenly moved at the speed of cars rather than the trot of horses meant that new laws had to be enacted, new infrastructures built, and new social norms developed.[1]

These two images are a good reason to pause for a moment to think seriously about the implications of sweeping, technology-driven change. Today we stand at the cusp of a new AI-driven revolution that is already changing how we live, work, communicate, and learn at the pace and scale that may be without precedent in human history.

For more than 250 years, technology innovation has been changing the nature of jobs and work. In the 1740s, the First Industrial Revolution began moving jobs away from homes and farms to rapidly growing cities. The Second Industrial Revolution, which began in the 1870s, continued this trend, and led to the assembly line, the modern corporation, and workplaces that started to resemble offices that we would recognize today. The shift from reliance on horses to automobiles eliminated numerous occupations while creating new categories of jobs that no one initially imagined. Sweeping economic changes also created difficult and sometimes dangerous working conditions that led governments to adopt labor protections and practices that are still in place today.

The Third Industrial Revolution brought information technology into the workplace. This changed how people communicated and collaborated at work. While it added new IT positions it largely eliminated jobs for secretaries who turned handwritten prose into typed copy.

With AI and the digitization of data, the nature of jobs and work is changing again. In their book "No Ordinary Disruption," authors Richard Dobbs, James Manyika, and Jonathan Woetzel estimate that change today is happening 10 times faster and at 300 times the scale of the First Industrial Revolution, which works out to about 3,000 times the impact.

The potential of AI and digitally driven change is so "vast and fast" that some are calling it the Fourth Industrial Revolution. The benefits are enormous. And so are the challenges, especially for healthcare. Accenture has created a "disruptability index," which analyzes disruption of smart technologies across 20 industries. Healthcare is among the top industries that will be significantly disrupted by AI.[2]

Today most health leaders are excited about the opportunities to use AI and smart systems to drive systemic change in keeping with their mission and goals. At the same time there is a growing recognition that their organizations are not adequately prepared for the industry disruption that lies ahead.

Preparing for, and navigating through, such change is not for the faint of heart. While some health leaders take a narrow view of AI by relegating it to being another technical improvement to be managed by capable IT leaders, the move towards becoming an Intelligent Health System requires leaders to think and act differently. Successful leaders will leverage AI to create new approaches in which an organization's activities, people, culture, and structure are aligned with the new expectations of the market.

At the heart of the "leadership imperative" is the recognition that, while the mission of your organization will remain the same, the means and manner in which you pursue and accomplish it will undergo a systemic change. From the lack of resources, talent, and the pull of competing priorities, there are many obstacles organizations will face in the quest to adopt AI. And while such issues are challenging, the single greatest predictor for success will be the presence of transformational leadership.

Are You a Change Master or Transformation Leader?

Organizations that claim to be "transforming" seem to be everywhere these days. Adding to this all of the articles and talks on the topic, you would think we would be really good at business and digital transformation. In reality, we are not. A study by McKinsey & company estimates that 70% of organizational transformation efforts fail.[3]

The high failure rate seen by most organizations likely comes from an inherent misunderstanding of the difference between change management versus true transformation. Ron Ashkenas, coauthor of the *Harvard Business Review Leader's Handbook*, describes "change management" as the implementation of finite initiatives that focus on executing a well-defined shift in the way things work. These may cut across an organization but can just as easily be confined to a division or a specific process.[4]

Transformation is another animal all together. Unlike change management, it's not focused on a set of discrete, well-defined shifts in how work is done. Instead it focuses on a diverse set of initiatives that are both interdependent and intersecting. Most importantly, the overall goal of transformation is not just to execute a defined change, but to reinvent the organization and discover a new or revised business model based on a vision for the future.

Compared to change management, transformation is much more unpredictable, iterative, and experimental. It entails a much higher risk. And even if successful change management leads to the execution of certain initiatives within the transformation portfolio, the overall transformation could still fail.[5]

And so, while new AI technologies may be catalysts for dramatic performance improvement, unlocking their true power comes from leaders who understand and commit to leading transformation rather than simply trying to manage change.

The transformative power of AI brings with it complicated challenges. These range from business disruption, security risks, to concerns of exacerbating inequalities, to the disruptive impact on your work force. Choosing to lead organizations on the AI journey requires leaders to recognize the difference between being change agents and transformational leaders. Those who choose the path of transformation will focus their efforts in three interconnected areas.

Reimagining Processes and Workflows

Don Berwick, MD, MPP, has always been an exemplar in the global movement to improve quality. As former Administrator of the Centers for Medicare and Medicaid Services and Chief Executive Officer of the Institute for Healthcare Improvement he was an early champion in the quality movement and remains a luminary in the quest to make healthcare better.

In writing the foreword to the book Transforming Healthcare (a great read on the groundbreaking work at Virginia Mason to apply lean Toyota Production System principles in health), Dr. Berwick notes "the word Transformation is much used in the stratosphere of quality improvement, but its meaning varies. The big idea, underlying all uses of the term, is that harvesting the full promise of modern system improvement methods requires much more than a mere catalog of projects. A hospital, let alone healthcare as a total system, is a monstrously complex organism – hundreds or thousands of processes ticking away all the time with thousands or tens of thousands of staff interacting among themselves with the equipment, patients, software and the relevant environment."[6]

It is against the background described by Dr. Berwick that transformational leaders begin to apply AI in health.

Begin your AI journey by assessing and selecting the clinical and operational workflow processes that are critical to success and also ripe for change. The key to success is a strategy that begins with a few initiatives where current processes will be improved by automation or augmentation through AI.

Processes first need to be defined. In health, there seems to be an expectation that AI will deliver the magic formula to cure everything. Yet when implementing such AI I often find that existing workflows have significant gaps that AI alone is unable to overcome alone.

It's also important to look beyond how things are done today. Done right, AI opens the door to reimagining new processes rather than simply automating existing processes. While automation often yields a short-term jump in productivity, such benefits will level off if the focus is on process automation rather than reinvention.

Transformational leaders use AI to reimagine and reinvent standard processes in keeping with the needs of consumers, clinicians, and staff. From creating more personalized care to improving throughput at the point of care, the pursuit of value from AI starts with reimagining processes and workflows.

Workforce Transformation

Transformational leaders recognize and act on the premise that the value AI comes down to unlocking the full potential of the continuous interactions between humans and machines. As predictive capabilities, interactive bots, and digital self-service come into play they will affect every aspect of clinical and operational workflows. Successfully creating and managing this transition requires that leaders actively identify relevant stakeholders, and bring along in this journey their clinicians, employees, patients, and consumers. This is done through redefining jobs, career paths, and retraining.

A global study by the Organization for Economic Co-operation and Development (OECD) across its 32 member countries notes that close to one in two jobs that exist today will be significantly affected by automation through AI.[7] Any successful AI plan must include how to best match people and machines as the decisions being made today will have a longtail effect on workforce composition, productivity, and operating margins for years to come.

Going forward, leaders will actively support the remaking of the organizational culture and help employees keep pace with the change that is occurring by articulating a new view of the future of work. More on this in the next chapter.

Data as a Strategic Asset

In an AI-driven world data is no longer just a byproduct of clinical and business processes. It's the new currency that moves the industry forward and the fuel that drives a continuous understanding and interaction with consumers and the new intelligent marketplace. Going forward, creating and managing your data estate will be as important to success as managing your finances and operational assets.

The idea behind developing and managing your data estate is to make sure all data resources are positioned in such a way that they can be used, shared, and moved easily and efficiently in service of improving internal and external processes.

Intelligent Health Systems require leaders to better understand how to curate and use all forms of data differently. Most often we confine our thinking about data to what we "control." These data assets include things like data from Electronic Health Records (EHRs), imaging, revenue cycle, and registration. Going forward creating and managing data estates for intelligent health will also include making greater use of other data residing outside your organization, including market demographics, social, and environmental determinant data. Such data is often readily available for use, but often overlooked by health organizations when planning and managing the organization's data estate.

Creating and managing a modern data estate to support AI and intelligent solutions will require different ways of operating. For example, the role and use of the cloud become critical to success as different types of data from diverse sources are bought together to drive planning and service delivery solutions. As data is used in new ways, including the development of predictive algorithms, a different set of ethical and legal risks are created that will need to be understood and managed. We go into detail in Chapter 11.

As our corporate data stores have grown in both size and subject area diversity, it has become clear that a strategy to address data is necessary. Yet some still struggle with the idea that corporate data needs a comprehensive strategy. More on this in Chapter 13.

The New Face of AI Leaders

In the world of AI and intelligent health, transformational leadership will require the following skills and characteristics.

Planning visionary

Effectively managing the introduction and pursuit of AI-driven transformation starts with defining a vision and then backing it up with razor-sharp clarity about the new market demands, future operating models, the rationale for why change is needed, and how success will be defined and measured.

Managing the introduction of a new AI-enhanced business model is important. Your approach should highlight your innovation goals which are usually broad. But in order to be meaningful and give direction to the whole organization, this should also include quantitative objectives that can translate to Key Performance Indicators (KPIs). Clear KPIs for the future business model allow management to maintain a constant perspective on the organization's progress toward its goals. In this regard they become a fundamental point of orientation for all AI planning and investments.

Planning visionaries do well when they focus on the end results. Move your focus to the end. As organizations begin to understand the many options for AI-driven transformation, they quickly realize that have more opportunities than they can pursue. Success will mean carefully choosing the specific opportunities your organization wants to target. Just as important your organization will decide which opportunities not to target. With these things in mind your planning process will work backwards to determine how to get started.

Strategically ambidextrous

Large-scale change and disruption are on the horizon as you move people and the organization into the next phase of intelligent health. Successful leaders understand this, and lead organizations to pursue a dual strategy. This includes protecting and repositioning core service lines that exist today while actively investing in transformation activities that seed the new growth opportunities in keeping with market and consumer demands. This pursuit of "two journeys" sets an organization in a new direction while recognizing that a transition period is needed to accommodate the move to new processes and ways of doing business.

For most organizations this dual transformation typically takes years. As the market is moving quickly, there's no time to waste in getting started. It's important to have a plan that includes a realistic timeline for making the transition. Ideally, an organization assesses its situation and adopts a plan that includes a "goldilocks" timeline. Not too fast which means the pursuit of an unrealistic set of expectations that won't be met, or too slow which puts your organization at risk of losing ground to competitors or new market entrants.

Customer obsessed

Shifting expectations are pushing health organizations to improve the consumer experience across all touchpoints. Excellence in one area is not sufficient as consumers expect the same frictionless experience across all interactions and touchpoints.

An obsession with improving the consumer experience is foundational to success in creating an Intelligent Health System. Leadership should aspire to evaluating and fixing every error or bad experience. Customers include your existing patients, consumers in the markets you serve, your medical staff, employees, and referral sources.

Internal evangelist

The single most important determinant in early success for enterprise-wide AI and intelligent heath is how effectively you bring everyone along in the move to reinvent the organization.

Transformational AI leaders understand that success is dependent on the effort of the entire team. This starts with the full commitment of clinical and business leadership. Leaders must understand and commit to a strategy and then actively communicate the importance and benefits of the strategy to all.

An important factor for driving cultural change and stimulating new growth is having all employees and constituents understand what is happening and why it is their interest as well as organizations to embrace the change that is occurring. In this regard an important role of leaders is to be effective storytellers. While your professional communications staff (human resources, public relations and, marketing) can support the packaging and positioning of change, organizational leaders must be on the frontlines to effectively communicate the "what and why" messages surrounding transformation.

Telling that kind of story about the future is not a one-time event. Leaders should be tireless, consistent, and persistent in bringing the core message home to all. Additionally, the message being delivered will need to be tailored to fit with the many internal constituents that will impact your success.

Agile adaptability

Transformational leaders must be prepared to think differently about how AI and intelligent systems change clinical and operational processes and be prepared to drive change. At times, setting aspirations that, on the surface, seem unreasonable may be a means of jarring an organization into seeing AI as a way of creating value in a changing marketplace.

Leaders of incumbent health systems must lead efforts that challenge the status quo rather than accepting historical norms. Assume there is an unknown company looking to enter the health space asking the same question as it plots to disrupt your organization's business or referral patterns. It is no coincidence that many textbook cases of companies redefining themselves come from Silicon Valley, the epicenter of digital disruption.

Tech and data enabled

AI done right will impact the organization's entire value chain. It will do this by taking different shapes and forms in different areas. Transformational leaders will need to invest in the right talent and a full set of AI tools and solutions. Additionally, leaders must understand that the technologies and the market are changing and should be prepared to keep up with rapid advancements.

From global health organizations to clinical divisions within a hospital and new entrants to the health sector, Intelligent Health Systems will come in all sizes and shapes. The glue binding them together will be leaders who understand and successfully leverage AI to address the changing market and consumer demands. While the tools and approach are different, the focus of such efforts is no different than what effective leaders have always championed: Improving quality and efficiencies while building greater loyalty amongst consumers and staff.

Just as we started this chapter, health organizations today face a world of uncertainty similar to an era where we relied on horses. Just as the world then didn't need better or faster horses, healthcare today doesn't need to create incremental efficiencies. The time for AI pilots and experimentation is coming to an end. Transformational leadership means creating an enterprise-wide plan that moves everyone forward.

IS YOUR BOARD AI SAVVY – FIVE QUESTIONS TO FIND OUT

As chair of the Board for Deloitte, a global company that provides audit, consulting, tax, and advisory services, Janet Foutty spends a lot of time working with organizational leaders and their boards to stay ahead of technology-driven changes in the market.

"I firmly believe that every company is a technology company. You have to be – to adapt to the disruptions that are coming in increasingly rapid waves," says Foutty. "Understanding, incorporating, and taking advantage of technology has become table stakes for every business or be left behind. Furthermore, I also believe that governing bodies and boards should play an important, even outsized role in helping their organizations gain a more holistic understanding of technology and strategy that extends beyond managing risk."

Beyond the role and responsibility clinical and business leaders in leading transformation through AI, an organization's governing or operation boards are ideally situated to help identify the optimal value and impact of technology investments; understand the ethical implications of digital design and use; and prepare for the talent implications brought about with the adoption and use of AI.

Foutty notes that not everyone on a board needs to be a technologist, but she believes that it's important for all members to gain a foundational understanding of, and be conversant in, the technologies that drive change and opportunity for the organization. This level of understanding also ties into the board's responsibility to monitor and advise whether the C-suite and senior management have the necessary technology skills.

To this end, Foutty suggests five key questions board chairs and members should ask of themselves – not only to drive their tech savviness but also to guide board conversations and strategy development at that very important intersection of technology, governance, and transformation.

1. **Are we thinking about opportunities or solely about risks?** A study reported that 48% of board conversations about technology are centered on cyber risk and privacy topics, while less than a third (32%) are concerned with digital transformation driven by technology. While it's critical for boards to understand technological risk, I believe they must spend equal time discussing the many strategic opportunities technology affords.
2. **Are technologists represented?** Adding a technologist to the board – for example, a current or former Chief Information Officer (CIO), Chief Technology Officer (CTO), or other C-level tech leader – can bring both new skill sets and fresh thinking to the boardroom as it relates to tech-related opportunities, risk, spending, and organizational strategy enablement.
3. **Are we committed to continuous learning?** The future of work requires *everyone* from the boardroom to the workforce at large to be committed to lifelong learning, given the rapid rate of disruption and change.
4. **Are we engaged with the office of the *CIO, CTO*, and Chief Data Officer (CDO)?** Whether through a designated committee or as a full

board, members should dive deeper on technology topics with subject matter experts outside the boardroom.

5. **Are we effectively identifying and managing the ethical implications of technology?** A true understanding of technology requires considering the ethical implications of where and how technology is being applied. This includes mitigating unintentional biases and consequences; creating a diverse and inclusive technology organization; and overseeing growing technology ecosystems beyond your organization. And, as both understanding and use of technology increases, the innately human skills, such as judgment and empathy, should remain at the center.

So, if every company is a tech company – every board is a tech board and must therefore focus on increasing their own tech savviness, and helping their organizations do the same. Not only should we ready ourselves for the impact of technology to better manage its risks, boards can (and should!) leverage its many opportunities.[8]

Notes

1 Modified and Used with Permission from a Cloud for Global Good, *Microsoft*, 2017.
2 Digital Health Tech Vision, Kaveh Safavi, Accenture Consulting, 2019, www.accenture.com/_acnmedia/PDF-102/Accenture-Digital-Health-Tech-Vision-2019.pdf#zoom=50.
3 70% of Transformation Programs Fail, AIPMM/McKinsey, 2013, www.slideshare.net/aipmm/70–26633757.
4 We Still Don't Know the Difference between Change and Transformation, Ron Ashkenas, *Harvard Business Review*, 2015.
5 Ibid.
6 Charles Kenney, *Transforming Health Care*, CRC Press, 2013.
7 Ljubica Nedelkoska, Glenda Quintini, "Automation, skills use and training", *OECD Social, Employment and Migration Working Papers*, No. 202, OECD Publishing, Paris, 2018.
8 Janet Foutty, Is your Board Tech Savvy? 5 Questions to Find Out, LinkedIn, 2019, www.linkedin.com/pulse/your-board-tech-savvy-5-questions-find-out-janet-foutty/?trackingId=jm%2BOAZM%2BvNVFM%2B6rJuP6NQ%3D%3D.

Chapter 8

When AI Meets HR

When it comes to sci-fi movies and novels, everyone loves a good "human versus machine" fight. From Hal 9000 in the movie *2001 A Space Odyssey* to Agent Smith, the creepy sentient in *The Matrix*, we've been conditioned to see smart machines as adversarial and something to fear.

The view of smart machines being adversarial or threatening is nothing new. It's also not limited to books and movies. Today, the number of people who fear their jobs are at risk from Artificial Intelligence (AI) and automation is growing.[1] This sentiment can be found in the hallways of healthcare organizations. Some of your best clinicians and staff are likely worried, or at least contemplating, the impact of AI on their work and careers.

While no one has a crystal ball to predict exactly what will happen, one thing is certain. As health organizations are increasingly AI-enabled, the disruption of your workforce is coming. It's also necessary to realize the value promised by AI.

The reality is that some jobs will be eliminated as new ones are created. Most important to your success will be managing how existing jobs will be transformed through the introduction and use of smart machines and systems. As the nature of work and employment changes through AI, transformational leaders will define and execute AI plans that evolve to create high-performance loops. These new types of workflows will take advantage of the synergies of human capabilities being enhanced by AI.

Whether a new grad, a "midcareer" millennial, or a physician in "wind-down" mode, it's a sure bet that AI will impact everyone at all levels of the organization. The question is not whether AI will reshape the workplace.

Instead the most important question for leaders is how to curate and successfully support workforce transformation.

In many organizations today the "AI meets HR" conversation is lagging behind the technology investments being made. Research from Accenture shows business leaders don't think workers are ready for AI and yet, only 3% of leaders were reinvesting in training. As a result, workers are not being adequately prepared for the future.[2]

From optimism in the C-suite to skepticism among in the ranks, AI usually generates strong reactions at all levels of an organization. Some believe in its seemingly unbridled potential while others see it as a career killer. As many as 84% of managers expect AI to make their work more effective and interesting. At the same time 36% are concerned that it will threaten their jobs.[3] When asked if they would be comfortable with AI monitoring and evaluating their work, 42% of top managers "strongly agree" with the statement. Only 26% of middle managers and 15% of frontline managers demonstrated the same level of enthusiasm.

Willingness to accept responsibility for intelligent machines' actions follows the same pattern, with top managers being most accepting and frontline managers being least (45% versus 17% "strongly agree," respectively).[4]

Similarly, age makes a difference when it comes to attitudes toward AI. When asked whether they would trust AI's advice while making decisions in the future, 33% of managers 35 years old and younger strongly agreed. Only 13% of managers over the age of 50 gave the same response.[5]

One of the greatest risks for any organization implementing an AI strategy comes when intelligent capabilities are inserted into an enterprise that is still optimized for the workforce of the past.

Realizing the value AI can deliver requires leaders to explore new operating models. This means managing not only the technical side of the AI but also the softer side of transformation. As predictive capabilities, interactive bots, and digital self-service come into play they will affect every aspect of clinical and operational workflows. Successfully creating and managing this transition requires that leaders actively plan to bring along their clinicians and employees, through redefining jobs, career paths, and retraining.

A successful AI plan must include how to best match people and machines, as the decisions being made today will have a longtail effect on workforce composition, productivity, and operating margins for years to come.

Understanding where and why change will occur and having a plan to address it is the key to success.

AI to the Rescue

Done right, the journey to become an Intelligent Health System will help solve one of the largest challenges currently facing most health organizations worldwide – The shortage of human capital. Whether it's playing employees to their highest value or ensuring your organization has sufficient human resources to keep up with the demand for health services, AI has to potential to solve many of the human capital problems facing healthcare today.

Healthcare is now the largest employer of workers in the United States. In 2000, there were 7 million more workers in manufacturing than in healthcare. At the beginning of the Great Recession, there were 2.4 million more workers in retail than healthcare. In 2017, healthcare surpassed both industries in total number of employees.[6]

In the United States healthcare employs 16 million workers representing one out of every eight jobs in America. Looking forward, five of the ten jobs that will see the fastest percentage growth in the next decade are in health. Health is projected to account for one-third of all new jobs during this period.[7]

And while these job statistics are good for the economy, this dramatic growth will not keep up with the demand for skilled health workers. A significant shortage in the workforce is coming.

Based on the growth of the aging population alone, the United States will need to hire 2.3 million new healthcare workers by 2025 just to keep up with the demand for services according to a study by Mercer.[8] This race against the clock is already being felt by provider organizations as thousands of positions are currently going unfilled due to lack of qualified workers (Figure 8.1).

Worldwide the story is the same. Today there is an estimated shortage of 7.2 million healthcare workers.[9]

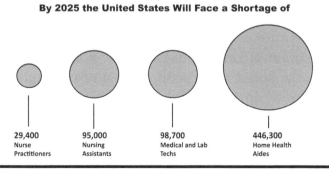

By 2025 the United States Will Face a Shortage of

| 29,400 | 95,000 | 98,700 | 446,300 |
| Nurse Practitioners | Nursing Assistants | Medical and Lab Techs | Home Health Aides |

Figure 8.1   US Workforce Shortage in Healthcare. (Mercer's US Healthcare Labor Market Analysis, Calculations by Mercer's Workforce Strategy and Analytics Practice.)

There will be 300 million more people aged 65 and over by 2030, creating a significant demand for not only clinicians but also a range of occupations, including community health workers, home-health aides, personal-care aides, and nursing assistants. Globally, it is estimated that healthcare jobs related to aging could grow by 50–85 million by 2030.[10]

As global demand grows, the industry faces stiff headwinds in attracting and retaining a workforce capable of delivering the services needed. These include an aging workforce with staff retiring or leaving for better paid jobs without being replaced, not enough younger workers choosing health careers, or being adequately trained.

It's against this backdrop of increasing demands on the traditional health system coupled by a growing shortage of qualified workers that AI and digital transformation can serve as the paradigm shift.

A study by McKinsey and Company showed that current technologies could automate 45% of the activities workers are paid to perform. Additionally, about 60% of all occupations could experience 30% or more of their work activities being automated.[11]

Another study concluded that healthcare has a technical potential for automation of about 36%, but the potential is lower for health professionals whose daily activities require expertise and direct contact with patients. This study noted that less than 30% of a registered nurse's activities could be automated. Meanwhile, jobs such as nursing assistants could be more fully automated as much of the work consists of gathering health information. Even some of the more complex activities that doctors perform, such as reading radiology scans, have the technical potential for automation.[12]

When looking at the worldwide impact of AI on the future of work in healthcare, a study by the Organisation for Economic Co-operation and Development (OECD) concludes that more than 40% of healthcare jobs can be automated.[13]

The implications of AI on healthcare's future workforce is a hotly debated topic. Most agree that the impact of substituting machines for activities done by humans in healthcare creates significant issues to be addressed. These include the elimination of jobs, rethinking how work is done, consumer expectations, and the social implication of what responsibilities an employer has to its employees when it comes to helping them transition to be part of an intelligent work environment.

Done right, the introduction and use of AI enables both cost-cutting automation of routine work and value-adding augmentation of human capabilities. Both require a careful assessment and actions that impact the workforce. In the context of managing such change, research and experience show that putting people first and amplifying what they can achieve in conjunction with intelligent machines holds the greatest potential for value creation within high-performance organizations.

Choose One: Divide or Empower Your Workforce

Just as the first Industrial Revolution drove automation of repetitive physical work, the intelligence revolution is having a similar effect on a wide range of intellectual activities that comprise the provision of health services today. As this occurs, employee resistance can become the single greatest barrier to the adoption of smart systems.

In a survey of health and IT leaders by Infosys, 57% of participants cited employee fear as the greatest barrier to adopting AI technology followed by lack of cultural acceptance (50%) and lack of inhouse skills (48%).[14] It's no wonder that employees and clinical staff are feeling insecure over the implementation of technology that could eliminate or at least change the nature of their work. In the same survey, one-third of organizations surveyed indicated that they had plans to replace workforce resources with smart technology in the coming year.

Today many organizations are unknowingly feeding a collective staff insecurity and creating a digital divide by not addressing human impact as a "front and center" issue in developing and deploying AI. Leaders endeavoring to avoid or close this gap are incorporating next-generation workforce plans into their AI technology adoption strategies. The addition of HR planning as an integral part of your organization's AI strategy helps to address the long-term needs of the enterprise.

The engagement of your human resource and medical staff leadership is crucial in creating plans that leverage AI to amplify the knowledge and expertise of your teams in keeping with your mission and goals. Here are some of the fundamentals to consider in aligning your people strategy with your AI strategy.

Adopt and Communicate a People-First Approach

It's impossible to pick up a professional journal or attend a conference today without reading or hearing about AI and its impact on the future of work and health services. In almost all cases the focus is on the technology and its ability to reduce the need for employees.

While AI will increasingly play a role in automating the delivery of health services, humans will continue to be in charge of work. With this in mind, ground your AI strategy by adopting and advocating a people-first approach. In most cases, this is nothing new. Healthcare has always been a people-intensive, staff-focused endeavor.

Are your employees ready to change? Employees are more apt to support change if they are ready to make changes. In your words and actions, communicate that replacing people with machines is not the goal of becoming an Intelligent Health System. Instead, focus on how the goal of AI and a move towards becoming an Intelligent Health System is to achieve your goals and mission. Position AI as an enabler to automate routine work while empowering workers to achieve more by augmenting their expertise and capabilities.

A strategy of putting people first and using AI to amplify what they can achieve provides a solid foundation around which to manage the transformation of your workforce.

A people-first strategy does not mean that jobs won't be eliminated or altered. When done right staff will understand the need for change as your organization brings forward the view that AI will allow smart machines to amplify the capacity and expertise of the people delivering care and services.

A people-first approach increases the likelihood that staff will be prepared for the change that's coming. Ideally your workers will come to see intelligent machines in the workplace as a digital colleague. As AI reduces the burden of repetitive activities of lower value it allows your staff to serve at higher levels that use their best skills.

Understand How and Where AI Will Impact Jobs and Careers

While many jobs will be impacted by AI, it's important to recognize AI will affect some jobs more than others. Jobs at the greatest risk of being eliminated, or less human-dependent, are those consisting of repetitive tasks that can be automated through computer skills like vision, speech, text recognition, and computation.

Examples of repetitive task jobs that are at the greatest risk for automation include middle managers, lower-level accountants, bookkeepers, registration, and business office staff. This brings us to the types of jobs that will be secure and in high demand. Such jobs are those that make use of reasoning, imagination, empathy, critical thinking, creativity, and problem-solving skills. Noted theoretical physicist Micho Kiku characterizes these as attributes needed to engage in Intellectual Capitalism.

Why will jobs requiring these skills be more secure and in demand? As noted in Chapter 5, while breakthroughs that allow computers to mimic human qualities such as vision, speech, and knowledge management are happening at record speed, no one has figured out how to instill machines with reasoning capabilities or common sense. These remain uniquely human characteristics.

Examples of job types in this category include physicians, nurses, social workers, lawyers, and employees with specialized knowledge or problem-solving skills such as revenue cycle staff.

While there is no current gauge or standard, it is possible to assess which employees and job types are at the greatest risk of job displacement. Initial assessment can be completed by using existing information found in the structure of your approach to job descriptions and job classifications.

Each job or occupation is typically comprised of multiple types of defined skills and activities. Such an assessment starts by examining jobs and job types to evaluate what percentage of a job's activities are repeatable or predictable versus the percentage of activities that are considered knowledge work.

McKinsey and Company cites examples of activities that are more or less susceptible to AI automation. Activities that are highly susceptible to AI automation include data collection and processing. Less susceptible are activities involving unpredictable physical work or interactions with patients and customers. Activities least susceptible include activities like knowing and applying specialized knowledge and managing others.[15]

By mining data found in your current HR systems, things such as a "jobs impact" heat map can be generated to begin to understand how an enterprise AI plan will impact your future people plan.

Understanding and mapping which jobs or occupations are susceptible to automation provides an opportunity to shape transitions for how work will be done differently in the future. It also allows the organization to begin to define a plan with options for transitioning employees from current roles into new roles.

Create a Learning and Development Plan That Supports Transformation

By incorporating training and learning needs into technology strategies, leading health organizations can best match employees with both current and future enterprise skills needed.

This, in turn, will drive engagement, ensuring that people have continuous access to opportunities for learning and growth.

The move towards an AI-enabled work environment is putting new pressures on the already existing workforce challenges. These include:

- Increasing demand for advanced technology skills plus cognitive skills such as critical thinking and complex information processing.
- Automation of human-driven processes means that some workers will likely need to change occupations.
- As intelligent machines are integrated more deeply into the workplace, workflows will change and require skill sets that allow employees to effectively interact and collaborate with smart systems.

Today, many of the traditional organizational training programs are limited in scope and focused on maintaining or improving on existing competencies. While some innovative training and development programs are emerging, new solutions that can match the scale of the challenge will be needed.

Scaling and reimagining job retraining and workforce skills development are key areas for investment for those organizations that successfully transition to become intelligent work environments. This includes the need for learning and development programs to be integrated into technology strategies.

Given the nature of change that is coming, your organization will need to explicitly define what commitments will be made to employees affected by automation and what level of investment will be made to transition your workforce.[16]

In a survey where health leaders were asked what their organizations planned to do with employees displaced by AI automation: 42% reported that employees would be redeployed within the same area and 34% would be retrained for a new role. Twenty-four percent reported that affected employees would become redundant.[17]

The good news is that most current employees are willing and able to adapt to new tools and approaches to work if given the opportunity to be retrained. Providing job retraining and enabling individuals to learn marketable new skills throughout their lifetime will be a critical challenge.

Midcareer retraining will become more important as the skill mix is needed for a successful career change. Organizations can take a lead in some areas, including on-the-job training and providing opportunities for workers to upgrade their skills.

Equally important to creating and maintaining a strong workforce is understanding the perspective of younger professionals you seek to attract and retain. For example, in a study of millennials and their attitudes towards a work environment, 40% ranked learning and development second only to salary as the most important benefit in deciding where to work.

Furthermore, millennials and younger generations will actually demand greater automation – given their familiarity with highly efficient tools enabling mobility, flexibility, and other benefits outside of the workplace. The frustration of archaic systems is actually enough to drive them to seek other opportunities.

Automation will transform the workplace for everyone, including senior management. The rapid evolution of technology can make harnessing its potential and avoiding its pitfalls especially complex for senior managers who have ascended to senior leadership roles by mastering the creation and management of organizational systems. Such roles will also undergo a significant change.

Align Recruiting and Retention Plans to the New Intelligent Work Environment

The key to creating a high-performing workforce in an AI-driven world is less about attracting and retaining employees who tech savvy and more about hiring employees who are *change ready*.

There are many skills that will be required around which employees will come into the organization prepared to deliver. It's easy to check the boxes on technical skills when hiring new talent. More importantly, it's harder to gauge a job candidate's aptitude for change and innovation. Innovative employers are increasingly embracing hiring practices that seek out and assess candidates that have the ability to fit within work environments that are dynamically changing.

Carol Dweck is a Stanford psychology professor that has popularized the notion of the growth mindset.[18] Simply put this theory puts people's attitudes into two categories. Those with a fixed mindset attitude believe they are who they are and cannot change. Someone with a growth mindset believes that their most basic abilities can be developed through dedication and hard work and that brains and talent are starting points. People with growth mindsets believe they can essentially grow their brain's capacity to learn and solve new problems.

Hiring people with a growth mindset means that, instead of hiring fixed talent, you are hiring people who will become more and more talented over time. As a result, improvement in your company will be continuous and more sustainable.

Such people are on a journey of continuous improvement. As a result, they are more likely to achieve their goals. In fact, they are likely to move the goal posts altogether. They won't give up as easily and more likely to find a way to solve complex problems, and teach themselves new methods. Employees with a growth mindset are more likely to value effort, determination, and improvement over any talents they perceive to have been born with. Once you know what to look for, hiring people with a growth mindset is not necessarily difficult.

The adoption of AI in the workplace is not without risk. But for those with a growth mindset and a healthy degree of curiosity, this movement produces greater upside than downside. By proactively leaning into AI-driven change early, you and your teams will be better positioned to take advantage of new jobs being created while being better empowered for the career path you are on.

As more processes are digitized in every part of an organization, leaders must think at a macrolevel about the entire enterprise. How do you hire today for a diminished workforce 10 years out? When more and more of your people are replaced by bots, how do you lead, enforce quality control, and audit? The key to navigating through the coming such change will be identifying and retaining (retraining) employees who are capable of making one transition after another.

Create a Data-Driven Culture

Harnessing the power of data through AI only happens if your clinicians and workforce understand and embrace its power and utility. At the heart of having a workforce leverage AI capabilities is how such change fits with the overall culture of the organization.

Today, most health leaders would like to see data used pervasively throughout their organizations. And while health is amassing large amounts of data across the organization, much of its potential goes unrealized because the culture of the organization does not value the use of such data in its daily activities. Central to the success of your AI strategy is the ability to establish and cultivate a data-driven culture. A data-driven culture can be defined as *an operating environment that seeks to leverage data whenever and wherever possible to enhance clinical and business efficiency and effectiveness.*[19]

A study of 40 digital transformation initiatives by BCG found that the proportion of companies reporting breakthrough or strong financial performance was five times greater (90%) among those that focused on culture than it was among those that neglected culture (17%).

A data-driven culture is as *an operating environment that seeks to leverage data whenever and wherever possible to enhance business efficiency and effectiveness.*

The case for fostering a digital and data culture is even more powerful if you look at sustained performance: nearly 80% of the companies that focused on culture sustained strong or breakthrough performance over a period of 3 years. Not one of the companies that neglected to focus on culture achieved such performance.[20]

A data-driven culture empowers people to deliver results faster. Intelligent health organizations move faster than traditional ones, and their flatter hierarchy helps speed decision-making. A digital culture serves as a code of conduct that gives employees the latitude to make judgment calls and on-the-spot decisions.

The creation of a data-driven culture does not happen overnight. It requires an ongoing commitment of time and effort and an investment of money. Recruiting the best data science team or buying the best smart technology contribute to the likelihood of success. More importantly, IT specialists and tools alone won't necessarily guarantee the transformation of a data-resistant culture. While all these different factors can contribute to creating a data-driven culture, one of the most influential factors is *executive buy-in and support.* Data-driven cultures begin at the top of any organization and cascade down into all levels of the organization.

If you and your leadership team are prepared to lead by example with data, there are several ways in which you can visibly demonstrate the importance of data to your organization. Modeling the desired behaviors through your own actions demonstrate the importance of data in public settings. Here are six areas where executives can lead by example with data:[21]

1. **Daily usage.** One of the most impactful ways of sending a message to your organization that data matters is for executives to actively use the data. While most busy leaders aren't likely to log into an advanced analytics tool, they could benefit from having a performance dashboard available and demonstrating routine use of available clinical and operational data.

2. **Decisions.** If data is truly important to your organization, all of your leaders' decisions should be based on data. When executives request data in order to make key decisions, they reinforce data's role as an important strategic asset that serves an integral part of the decision-making process. They can also hold their direct reports accountable to use data in their decision-making.

3. **Communications.** Each email, presentation, or meeting discussion represents an opportunity to share insights on business performance, promote data-driven wins, and emphasize data's importance to the organization.

4. **Meetings.** Executives spend between 40% and 50% of their time in meetings. Many of these meetings can be time-consuming and ineffective. However, if a greater emphasis is placed on reviewing key metrics and developing action plans based on the results, data can then guide the meeting agenda and make meetings more focused, productive, and useful for everyone involved.

5. **Training.** Where busy executives choose to spend their time can indicate how important something is to them. When executives carve out time to participate in data skills training, it sends a powerful message to their team that these skills will be critical to success.

Paul Daugherty is the author of a great book about the interplay and impact of AI and humans aptly called *Humans + Machines*. Based on research drawn from how AI can strengthen productivity, enable innovation, and increase efficiency, Daugherty thinks that one of the biggest problems with AI today is the belief that AI will make human jobs redundant while missing the key point that when done right AI will make our working life better.

Smart leaders in health recognize that the goal of AI is not to replace people with machines but rather how to bring the two together in an effective collaboration that drives success. Or as Daugherty sums up the opportunity: "Humans plus machines equals superpowers."

Notes

1 Carol Stubbings, Jon Williams, Bhushan Sethi, Justine Brown, Workforce of the Future: The Competing Forces Shaping 2030, *PwC*, 2017, www.pwc.com/gx/en/services/peopleorganisation/publications/workforce-of-the-future.html.
2 Vegard Kolbjørnsrud, The Promise of Artificial Intelligence-Redefining Management in the Workforce of the Future, Accenture, 2016, www.accenture.com/us-en/insight-promise-artificial-intelligence.
3 file:///C:/Users/tomlawry/OneDrive%20-%20Microsoft/AI%20Book/Chapters/AI%20meets%20HR/AI_in_Management_Report.pdf.
4 Ibid.
5 Ibid.
6 Derek Thomson, Health Care Just Became the U.S.'s Largest Employer, *The Atlantic*, 2018, www.theatlantic.com/business/archive/2018/01/health-care-america-jobs/550079/.
7 Ibid.
8 Mathew Stevenson, Demand for Healthcare Workers Will Outpace Supply by 2025-An Analysis of the US Healthcare Labor Market, Mercer HPA, 2018, www.mercer.us/our-thinking/career/workforce-for-the-future/demand-for-healthcare-workers-will-outpace-supply-by-2025.html.
9 Global Health Workforce Shortage to Reach 12.9 million in Coming Decades, WHO, 2013, www.who.int/mediacentre/news/releases/2013/health-workforce-shortage/en/.
10 Jobs Lost Jobs Gained-Workforce Transitions in a Time of Automation, McKinsey Global Institute, 2017, www.mckinsey.com/featured-insights/future-of-work/jobs-lost-jobs-gained-what-the-future-of-work-will-mean-for-jobs-skills-and-wages.
11 Michael Chui, Where Machines Could Replace Humans-and Where They Can't, McKinsey & Company, 2017, www.mckinsey.com/business-functions/digital-mckinsey/our-insights/where-machines-could-replace-humans-and-where-they-cant-yet.
12 Ibid.
13 L. Nedelkoska, G. Quintini, "Automation, skills use and training", *OECD Social, Employment and Migration Working Papers*, No. 202, OECD Publishing, Paris, 2018. https://doi.org/10.1787/2e2f4eea-en.
14 AI for Healthcare-Balancing Efficiency and Ethics, Infosys, 2017, www.infosys.com/smart-automation/Documents/ai-healthcare.pdf.

15 Michael Chui, Where Machines Could Replace Humans-and Where They Can't, McKinsey & Company, 2017, www.mckinsey.com/business-functions/digital-mckinsey/our-insights/where-machines-could-replace-humans-and-where-they-cant-yet.

16 AI, Automation and the Future of Work-Ten Things to Solve for, McKinsey and Company, www.mckinsey.com/featured-insights/future-of-work/ai-automation-and-the-future-of-work-ten-things-to-solve-for, 2018.

17 AI for Healthcare-Balancing Efficiency and Ethics, Infosys, 2017, www.infosys.com/smart-automation/Documents/ai-healthcare.pdf.

18 Shana Lebowitz, A Stanford Psychologist Explains What Managers Can Learn from a Baseball Team's Interviewing Process, Business Insider, www.businessinsider.com/carol-dweck-explains-how-to-hire-people-with-growth-mindsets-2016-1/, 2016.

19 Brent Dykes, Creating a Data-Driven Culture: Why Leading by Example Is Essential, *Forbes*, 2017, www.forbes.com/sites/brentdykes/2017/10/26/creating-a-data-driven-culture-why-leading-by-example-is-essential/#d5cf6ad6737f.

20 Jim Hemerling, Julie Kilmann, Martin Danoesastro, Liza Stutts, Cailin Ahern, It's Not a Digital Transformation Without a Digital Culture, *BCG*, 2018, www.bcg.com/publications/2018/not-digital-transformation-without-digital-culture.aspx.

21 Brent Dykes, Creating a Data-Driven Culture: Why Leading by Example Is Essential, *Forbes*, 2017, www.forbes.com/sites/brentdykes/2017/10/26/creating-a-data-driven-culture-why-leading-by-example-is-essential/#d5cf6ad6737f.

Chapter 9

Engaging Your Clinicians

It was 1919 when American physician William J. Mayo teamed up with his brother Charles Horace Mayo to found what is now the famed Mayo Clinic. The focus of their practice was on early health management rather than just treating those who were ill. Along the way William Mayo's expressed his vision by stating, "The aim of medicine is to prevent disease and prolong life, the ideal of medicine is to eliminate the need of a physician."[1]

It is likely that if Dr. Mayo were around today, he would be a strong proponent of Artificial Intelligence (AI) to achieve his vision of better health. And while the purpose of AI is not to eliminate the need for physicians, it certainly has the power to give them back time and empower them with greater capabilities to do good.

AI is reinventing healthcare as we know it. Look closely at the vignettes in this book and you see it's already happening. Nowhere will this change have a greater impact than on the physicians, nurses, and other clinicians who manage diagnostic, prescription, and monitoring activities. Going forward, many of these processes will be replaced or augmented by smart hardware, software, and testing.

This convergence of human and artificial intelligence is creating the opportunity to achieve "high-performance medicine" according to Eric Topol, MD, Department of Molecular Medicine, Scripps Research Institute and author of the best-selling book *Deep Medicine*. High-performance medicine leverages AI as its foundation by processing massive amounts of information quickly with outputs that increase the accuracy and applicability over time. It will not be devoid of human interaction and input, but more reliant on data technology. As AI alters the approach and activities taken by clinicians, Topol believes that healthcare will become more scientific and consistent in providing better-quality services at lower costs. In the long run, this will elevate the practice of medicine and patient health.

The effective transition to AI-enabled systems requires robust leadership. Much of this leadership should be focused on physicians and nurses. Physicians and nurses make most of the frontline decisions that determine the quality and efficiency of care. Equally important is that they also possess the experiential knowledge and the clinical skills to guide health organizations in making sound strategic choices in deploying AI in ways which impact the longer term patterns of service delivery.

Health organizations that are serious about transforming through AI must harness the energy and wisdom of their clinicians. Without the active engagement of clinicians, even the most technically correct implementation of data and AI solutions will be insufficient in driving the changes needed to deliver on your performance goals nor will such change likely be sustainable.

The Opportunities and Challenges of Clinician Engagement

Achieving a high level of engagement with clinicians in planning and deploying AI starts with understanding their views and attitudes about AI. It's then about engaging them in meaningful ways to ensure their alignment with the strategy and direction being taken by the organization.

From a planning perspective, the growing capabilities and use of AI in healthcare will continually improve data-gathering techniques. As this happens the better use of all types of data will lead to health and medical services being more personalized, precise, and consistent. As this scenario plays out, its value will come from augmenting the ways in which clinicians interact with their patients.

Additionally, many new findings and discoveries will come about as the capabilities of AI go beyond those of clinicians in sifting through massive volumes of data to discover unique insights about a patient's condition. In the future, hundreds of thousands of data points may go into diagnosing a condition and monitoring the progress of a treatment, therapy, or prescription. When AI is done right within an organization the goal is to increase rather than diminish the role and work done by clinicians. It will amplify the unique skills and attributes of clinicians that cannot be replicated by smart technologies. The primary goal of AI in health is to empower clinicians allowing them to operate at higher levels of expertise. This change will come about in several ways.

First, machine learning will dramatically improve the ability of health professionals to improve processes such as establishing a prognosis. Current prognostic models, such as the Acute Physiology and Chronic Health Evaluation (APACHE), score is restricted to only a handful of variables, because humans must enter and tally the scores. But large amounts of data drawn directly from Electronic Health Records (EHRs), claims databases, and other systems could allow new models using thousands of richer predictive variables.[2]

Second, AI will displace or enhance certain types of repetitive work in specialties such as radiology and anatomical pathology. These specialties have a high degree of work tasks that focus largely on interpreting digital images, which can now be fed directly to algorithms instead. In the future massive imaging data sets, combined with recent advances in computer vision, will drive rapid improvements in performance. As machine learning accuracy begins to exceed that of humans in performing certain tasks, radiologists and others will be freed from highly repetitive tasks and focus on higher value activities. More on the impact of AI on radiologists in the next chapter.

Other areas already being affected include patient safety, monitoring and interpreting streaming physiological data, and automating certain aspects of anesthesiology and critical care.[3]

Third, AI will improve diagnostic accuracy. A recent Institute of Medicine report highlighted the alarming frequency of diagnostic errors and the lack of interventions to reduce them. Algorithms will soon generate differential diagnoses, suggest high-value tests, and reduce overuse of testing.[4] From lab and imaging studies to the increasing use of "omics" data, medicine has always required clinicians to handle enormous amounts of data.

As the data explosion in health continues, AI will make use of this data to become an indispensable tool for clinicians seeking to better understand their patients. As patients' conditions and medical technologies become more complex, the role of AI will grow, and clinical medicine will be challenged to grow with it. This challenge will create winners and losers amongst clinicians and the health organizations in which they practice. A key success factor will be engaging clinicians early and making it easy and compelling for them to see AI as an opportunity rather than a threat.

Engaging Clinicians to Shape the Future before It Arrives

When it comes to the adoption and use of smart technologies many clinicians are feeling a bit insecure these days. Most understand that AI will change the way healthcare works but don't know explicitly how it will affect their work. In the absence of such information some worry about the threat of being replaced by machines.

Other clinicians base their view of how AI will impact them based on their experience with the advent and use of EHRs. Few doctors found the early iterations of EHRs to be helpful in patient care or in making them more effective or efficient. Many initially viewed EHRs as an imposition and an inevitable consequence of progress.

While there is little doubt that AI will have widespread impact in transforming the patient experience and clinicians' daily routines, many are concerned about how it will impact their autonomy, professional stature, and income. Some already struggle to care for an endless stream of patients who want to be seen, and at the same time, constantly hear in the media that much of what they do is a waste.

Physician burnout is also on the rise as four of ten physicians report feeling dissatisfied in their medical practice. Additionally, most physicians don't have a clear understanding of AI and how to apply current and future capabilities to benefit their patients and their practices. It's no wonder that these and other factors leave clinicians feeling overwhelmed and ill-equipped to implement change according to a study by McKinsey.[5]

It's against this backdrop that winning the support of clinicians is an important and at times tricky dance. Effectively engaging clinicians throughout the planning and implementation process decreases the risk of them feeling like victims or casualties of change, and instead, allows them to be active participants in not only shaping the future but defining their roles before it arrives.

Steps for Meaningful Clinician Engagement

Clinician engagement as a formal part of your AI plan is as important as getting the technology right. The goal is to engage clinicians in thinking deeply about what they see, that if changed with AI, would serve to dramatically improve the performance of the things they consider important.

This is most often focused on the quality and effectiveness of health and medical services.

With this in mind a great conceptual starting point for engaging clinicians comes from the book *Machine, Platform, Crowd: Harnessing Our Digital Future*. Written by MIT economists Andrew McAfee and Erik Brynjolfsson, they capture the emerging role of humans and AI with the modification of a question made famous by US President John F. Kennedy: "So we should ask not 'What will technology do to us?' but rather 'What do we want to do with technology?'"[6] By focusing your initial dialogues with clinicians on how AI planning activities support clinical priorities such as improving outcomes and the consumer experience, you create an opportunity to engage and enlist the top constituents on whom the success of any AI initiative rides.

Here are things to consider in helping to gain buy-in. These recommendations for clinician engagement for AI are based on a modified version of the Institute for Healthcare Improvement's framework of six elements that has proven to be successful in encouraging physician buy-in for large-scale shared quality initiatives.[7]

Define or Discover the Common Purpose: The first step in strategic AI transformation among clinicians is to clarify a set of goals that encourage a cultural shift to think as a system instead of in silos. Organizational-wide AI conversations often start by broadly defining technology capabilities and then move to an even broader characterization of how this will affect future clinical and operational work processes. While such conversations ground clinicians in an overall vision, they often leave them confused and on their own to figure out how such change will affect them.

Shift the focus of such discussions. Start with a collective look at market trends and AI capabilities that are unfolding and define how such changes will impact both the organization and the role and work of clinicians. With this as a springboard, engage physicians and nurses in defining organizational opportunities that focus on the use of AI to do something positive, noble, or important. The goal should be to define an actionable vision for how AI will be used in support of the organization's mission and goals. If done right, this becomes a shared vision around which a plan is built and executed.

Key to getting the buy-in of clinicians in a shared vision is providing a systematic analysis of market forces and realities. The next step is to collectively assess the organization's readiness and ability to leverage AI to achieve and sustain performance improvement. Even if there is resistance or mistrust, the goal should be to unite under a common purpose and plan.

When it comes to a common purpose, improving patient care is almost always at the core of any change agenda that clinicians will embrace.

Adopt an Engaging Style and Talk About Rewards and Benefits: Even if the organization's noble shared purpose resonates deeply with clinicians, they will also care intensely about how the changes brought about by AI will affect the way they practice as well as professional stature, job security, and income. As part of this, it's important to recognize that physicians, like everyone else, are at least motivated by financial incentives and career security.

Engage clinicians in ways that allow them to explore how AI can be used to augment and extend their skills and strengths. In the proper context AI can make up for human deficiencies and variation while amplifying strengths. Helping clinicians understand this dynamic and how AI can be used in service of their practices will hopefully empower them to do more than they do now.

For example, in a study of serious misdiagnosis-related harm, researchers found that three-fourths of all harm-related cases occur in the "Big Three" areas of vascular, infections, and cancer. Additionally, the study notes that in 82% of cases where patients are harmed were attributable to errors in clinical judgment.[8] The use of machine learning to assist clinicians in reducing variance in clinical judgment is just one example of how AI could be used to improve care delivery. Other opportunities include elimination of repetitive and low value activities, improved quality as AI augments areas such as clinical decision support, and improved time management.

The acceptance and ready adoption of the benefits of AI varies among clinicians and can sometimes be gauged by traditional dynamics like how long a physician has been in practice. Newly minted clinicians are coming out of training programs expecting to have access to intelligent systems. Clinicians who have been practicing for a while may not be as readily adaptable to what is occurring in the use of AI.

Treat Clinicians as Planning and Decision-Making Partners: Beyond engaging clinicians in planning activities, include them in the decision-making process. For example, let physicians lead the various aspects of planning, such as assessing and selecting which clinical use cases are chosen and deployed. This should be done in collaboration with your IT and data leadership in keeping with explicit selection criteria that balance investments, project complexity, and returns. Embed clinicians in the teams that are responsible for implementing specific clinical improvement initiatives. Engage their intellect in other nonclinical activities that have impact on the overall success of your AI strategy. Such opportunities include participation in data modernization planning or in developing your organization's protocols and policies for the ethical deployment and use of AI.

Segment the Engagement Plan and Provide Education: Identify early adopters and champions for AI and engage them as advocates throughout the organization. Find the frontline staff who are seen as leaders and actively educate them about the goals for AI-driven improvement efforts. Also, provide these clinicians with early access to training and orientation activities to help them gain skills for managing their own work through intelligent systems.

Use "Engaging" Improvement Methods by Using Data: One of the key elements to increasing clinician buy-in is to use data sensibly and focus on achieving improved performance objectives first. Define Key Performance Indicators for early pilots and routinely report progress against the goals that have been established. As such project show benefit, even if the improvements haven't been perfect, clinicians will realize that such projects are a part of an iterative process.

If You Don't Engage Your Clinicians Their Patients Will

Despite many innovative advances in medicine and technology, healthcare sometimes falls short at the fundamental job of most businesses: to reliably deliver what its customers need *on their terms*. In the face of the ever-increasing complexity of the health market, and the growing demands and expectations of health consumers, even the best intentions and hard work of individual physicians will not guarantee their success if they fail to take into account the changes already occurring through AI.

The transformation of healthcare through AI has begun. Many of the early changes being seen are driven by consumers and new market entrants rather than by the clinicians and health organizations that have traditionally served the market. As patients and consumers make greater use of smart apps and seek out services that best fit what they need on their terms they will reshape the current role of physicians. They will do this through the use of a variety of consumer-driven sensors and devices which allow them to become the "CEO of his or her own health" without coordinating with their physician, hospital, or care team. This will be particularly empowering in cases where patients have very little access to care or with populations that choose not to conform to the traditional payer–provider model.

Organizations that succeed in the world of Intelligent Health Systems will be those that actively use AI to support physicians and nurses in living up to their aspirations as caregivers. By actively engaging clinicians in the planning and development process you automatically increase your ability to improve efficiency, deliver the best outcomes, and retain and recruit the best people.

When it comes to engaging your clinicians in your AI strategy there's a small lesson to be learned in considering the definition of the word "diagnosis." It come from the Greek word and is defined simply as "knowing apart." In a sense, the use of machine learning and algorithms makes us better at distinguishing clinical differences, such as knowing a healthy cell versus a cancerous cell. In looking ahead, the value of increasing our diagnostic, or knowing apart capabilities, will come about when delivered in the context of fully engaged clinicians who add their human knowledge and wisdom to "knowing together."

NOVANT HEALTH AND THE JOURNEY TOWARDS INTELLIGENT HEALTH

Before Eric Eskioglu became a neurosurgeon, he was an engineer working for Boeing designing airplanes. To meet "Dr. E", as he likes to be called, is to understand the meaning of perpetual curiosity.

Today, Dr. Eskioglu is the executive vice president and chief medical officer at Novant Health, which consists of 640 care locations, including 15 hospitals and hundreds of outpatient facilities and physician clinics servicing patients in Virginia, North Carolina, South Carolina, and Georgia.

Having started its AI program in 2018, Novant Health is relatively new in its journey towards intelligent health but is making major strides in moving from aspiration to execution in its enterprise-wide approach to AI. Armed with a clear vision and strong executive sponsorship from the CEO and board, Dr. Eskioglu was asked to lead AI efforts for clinical transformation in partnership with Angela Yochem, Novant's chief digital and tech officer who had recently been recruited from outside the healthcare industry because of her deep digital transformation experience. They use AFECT (Alignment, Focus, Execution, Celebration, and Transformation) as their thought process for approaching AI.

"The first step we took in planning was to work at ensuring strategic and programmatic alignment amongst clinical and technology leaders in the organization. Developing such alignment started with working to "leave our egos at the door" to create an actionable strategic vision for how AI would be developed and used in service to our mission as well as our clinical and business goals."

With the vision and general plan in place the next phase in using AI to improve clinical services was educating and getting alignment amongst the clinical thought leaders in the organization.

"Novant has a strong physician-driven culture. Building up understanding and acceptance of our vision for how AI would be used to improve clinical processes and outcomes meant spending several months developing and telling the story of what AI is and how Novant Health would be using it to change the way services are provided in conjunction with the practice patterns of our clinicians," says Dr. Eskioglu. "We spent a lot of time making sure those communicating about our plan for AI stayed on a consistently focused message with a heavy emphasis on addressing the 'what and why' of our plan."

As the focusing phase to curate interest and support among clinical leaders peaked, Novant developed and delivered a 1 day AI for clinicians workshop with activities split between educating clinical leaders about AI and its uses within healthcare and planning activities designed to solicit clinical use cases to be considered as part of the initial AI pilots to be run by the organization. At the end of the session clinical leaders participating in the program identified more than 30 clinical use cases that were then prioritized by the group based on criteria to gauge clinical safety, quality, complexity, and costs for each use case.

"While we knew AI was an important topic, we were frankly surprised by level of commitment and participation by our clinical leaders. As the six-hour session was ending many of our physicians did not want to leave and instead kept the planning conversations going. Following this meeting the next step was to appoint a subset of physicians who participated in the planning event to further review all use case ideas generated and to recommend the top five clinical use case to be pursued based on a deeper set of evaluation criteria. From this clinician-driven process Novant selected its first two clinical pilots to pursue," says Dr. Eskioglu.

As the clinical execution process got underway an important parallel process continued to make Novant Health's technology and data estate "AI-Ready." This process, led by the chief digital and tech officer, Angela Yochem, created a modern, flexible, and on-demand solution set to provide for the consistent and secure delivery of AI-related services for clinical as well as operational and consumer-facing solutions.

In the summer of 2019 Novant brought together its work and learnings in the pursuit of becoming an Intelligent Health System by establishing the Institute of Innovation & Artificial Intelligence. The institute is focused on the advanced technologies required to provide highly personalized care and accelerated solutions with actionable data and insights for preventive prediction, diagnosis, and treatment to Novant Health's patients. Novant Health team members rotate in and out of the institute as subject matter experts on an as-needed basis while others have full-time assignments.

"Our focus with the Institute is to create a set of processes and constructs that allow team members from all parts of Novant Health to explore and experiment with emerging AI-based capabilities, acting as a distributed team, for the benefit of our patients and communities. As we build our competencies in AI and machine learning, we want our team members, business partners, and providers to have a place where they can present their ideas to improve the delivery of care." says Dr. Eskioglu.

Dr. Eskioglu and Angela Yochem are entering the celebration and look-back phase of AI at Novant Health. The successes of the institute are important, but so are the experiments and learnings gathered along the way. They look forward to continued transformation across the organization driven by advances in AI-based solutions and enabling superior patient safety, quality, and experience outcomes.

Notes

1 Peter Zhegin, Evgeniya Konovalova, The Role of AI in the Future of Health Care, Venture Beat, 2017, https://venturebeat.com/2017/07/19/the-role-of-ai-in-the-future-of-health-care/.
2 Ziad Obermeyer, M.D., Ezekiel J. Emanuel, M.D., Ph.D, Predicting the future—big data, machine learning, and clinical medicine, *The New England Journal of Medicine*, 2016, https://cdf.nejm.org/register/reg_multistep.aspx?promo=ONFGMM02&cpc=FMAAALLV0818B.
3 Ibid.
4 Ibid.
5 Pooja Kumar, MD, Anna Sherwood, Saumya Sutaria, MD, Engaging Physicians to Transform Operational and Clinical Performance, McKinsey and Company, 2017, http://healthcare.mckinsey.com/sites/default/files/MCK_Hosp_MDSurvey.pdf.
6 Andrew McAfee, Erik Brynjolfsson. *Machine, Platform, Crowd: Harnessing Our Digital Future*. W.W. Norton Publishing, 2017.
7 James L. Reinertsen, Alice G. Gosfield, William Rupp, John W. Whittington, "Engaging physicians in a shared quality agenda", *IHI Innovation Series White Paper*, Institute for Healthcare Improvement, Cambridge, MA, 2007, www.ihi.org/resources/Pages/IHIWhitePapers/EngagingPhysiciansWhitePaper.aspx.
8 David E. Newman-Toker, Adam C. Schaffer, C. Winnie Yu-Moe, Najlla Nassery, Ali S. Saber Tehrani, Gwendolyn D. Clemens, Zheyu Wang, Yuxin Zhu, Mehdi Fanai and Dana Siegal, Serious Misdiagnosis-Related Harms in Malpractice Claims: The "Big Three" – Vascular Events, Infections, and Cancers, DE Gruyter, 2019, www.degruyter.com/view/j/dx.ahead-of-print/dx-2019-0019/dx-2019-0019.xml.

Chapter 10

Making Radiologists More Rad

I was recently asked by the CEO of one of North America's premier pediatric medical centers to do a half-day Artificial Intelligence (AI) education session with its top clinical and operational leaders. As people were gathering before the start of the meeting, a group of physicians was already cloistered at a table sipping coffee. Their usual collegial banter was in full swing. Given the topic of the session, the Medical Director for Radiology was the subject of some razzing by his peers about the likelihood of AI putting radiologists out of business. "Have you thought about applying for a license to drive for Uber?" quipped a tablemate.

When it comes to the impact of AI in medicine, radiology may be the Rodney Dangerfield of medical specialties. It just doesn't get the respect it deserves.

Today, great strides are being made to leverage AI by embedding intelligence into the field of medical imaging to automate and streamline diagnostic processes. Each activity is carried out tens of thousands of times each day. In this regard, medical imaging is in the vanguard for how AI will disrupt the existing ways in which specialty health services are provided. Such change is driving us to reimagine the role of radiologists.

Radiology is an early example of how all specialties will need to define how humans best join forces with smart machines and systems. We'll use this chapter to highlight the current state of affairs in how AI is impacting radiology, recognizing that what's happening in this medical discipline is a proxy for every specialty. Each will go through a process of evaluating and changing how work will be done in the future.

Radiology Is Dead. Long Live Radiology

Immense progress is being made in the use and utility of machine learning (predictive capabilities) and vision AI (ability to recognize patterns and objects within pictures and images) in health and medicine. Radiology is a specialty undergoing rapid change as a result of the application of AI. As this occurs there are AI and clinical leaders that believe humans will soon be factored out of the equation in specialty areas like radiology.

A *New England Journal of Medicine* article in 2016 predicted that "machine learning will displace much of the work of radiologists and anatomical pathologists." [1] Shortly after this was published, Geoffrey Hinton, a rock star cognitive psychologist and computer scientist who splits his time between Google and the University of Toronto, noted that the impact of AI in the real world made it "quite obvious that we should stop training radiologists" as image perception algorithms were moving towards being demonstrably better than humans. Radiologists are, he said, "the coyote already over the edge of the cliff who hasn't yet looked down".[2]

Piling onto this frame of mind was Andrew Ng, another AI superstar researcher, who when discussing AI's ability to diagnose pneumonia from chest X-rays, wondered whether "radiologists should be worried about their jobs".[3]

In many respects *parts* of these forward-looking statements have come true. A growing number of studies and evidence are proving that AI can measurably outperform humans in critically important diagnostic tasks that are currently the purview of radiologists and radiology techs (this also spills over to any discipline making use of images including pathology, ultrasound, ophthalmology, and other specialties).

A recent study published in *Nature Medicine* notes that an algorithm was able to outperform radiologists in determining whether patients had lung cancer. The predictive capabilities of a smart machine detected 5% more cancers compared to human experts and also reduced false positives by 11%.[4] Another study published in the *Journal of the National Cancer Institute* noted that the use of AI in breast screenings performed at the same level as radiologists.[5] And, in yet another study, AI surpassed the performance of 58 international dermatologists in diagnosing skin cancers.[6]

And so, the use of AI in radiology clearly holds great promise in improving quality and operational effectiveness. Equally important to recognize is that it has the power to supplant, or at least augment, the capabilities of radiologists when focused on certain aspects of image analysis and diagnosis. Most importantly, and as noted in other chapters of this book, the application of AI capabilities to the provision of health and medical services in the real world is more complicated and nuanced than what many studies and articles point out.

Much of what is reported in the use of AI in medical imaging (including the studies cited above) depicts the potential of AI to affect one important but narrow aspect in the diagnostic workflow process. These studies and reports usually omit most other aspects of the work done by radiologists that could also be improved by AI. The stereotype of radiologists sitting all day in a darkened room "reading" images and dictating reports grossly underrepresents the role these specialists play. In reality radiologists provide a diverse set of services and knowledge and guidance to dozens of specialties whose diagnostic and treatment decisions are dependent.

Beyond reading and interpreting images radiologists are multidisciplinarians. Their work and expertise touch most aspects of inpatient care and many aspects of outpatient care with their contribution directly affecting quality, outcomes, and cost-effectiveness. This includes deciding which images should be taken, creating treatment plans in conjunction with specialists they support, conferring and advising on unusual or complex diagnoses, participating in tumor boards, teaching and training and many other things that AI cannot do to fit into the sometimes messy business of delivering medical care in the real world.

As noted in Chapter 4, we will continue to make use of "narrow AI" in the foreseeable future, which allows it to be used in automating or improving *very specific processes*. And as we learned in Chapter 5, there are many aspects in the provision of health and medical services that are fully dependent on human capabilities such as wisdom, judgment, and empathy. All of these dynamics come into play when we look at how radiologists are not victims of AI but rather early beneficiaries. In looking at what is already occurring in the medical imaging space, the opportunities to dramatically reinvent how radiologists work are pretty amazing.

It Takes a Village – Or at Least a Forward-Looking Medical Association

A great place to start in pursuit of AI innovation is to shift the focus from whether AI will replace humans in *doing a job* to how it will replace humans or make humans better at *performing specific tasks*. In this regard, improving diagnostic capabilities remains front and center in the application of AI in service of clinicians and consumers.

With this in mind, the American College of Radiology (ACR) not only helps its members understand and embrace AI but also encourages its use with the introduction of the ACR Data Science Institute and a groundbreaking free software platform that empowers radiologists to participate in the creation, validation, and use of healthcare AI (ACR AI-LAB). This platform provides radiologists with tools to develop AI algorithms at their own facilities, using their own data, to meet their own clinical needs.[7]

Beyond the technical aspects and benefits of its AI Lab, the initiative combines ACR's vast member network, its institutional connectivity to facilities, and a growing industry community that will collectively lead the industry's efforts to advance AI in health care.

This move is indicative of the power of clinical and health leaders to collaboratively leverage AI as a change agent. Instead of radiologists being marginalized they are reinventing their practices by "democratizing" AI through the direct participation of radiologists and radiology departments in the full AI development lifecycle. Radiologists who choose to participate are able to learn about AI, contribute AI data sets, share AI algorithms, evaluate AI models, develop AI models, and even combine these models through transfer learning and model ensembles to address their local clinical needs while making AI-driven diagnostic improvements available to all.

In creating an AI platform specific to medical imaging the ACR is creating a new community for radiologists to not only collaborate but also help solve for a key issue in the industry which is the creation and use of data sets on which everyone can benefit. As noted by Keith Dreyer, DO, PhD, Chief Science Officer. "Acquiring the necessary large amounts of patient data for algorithm training has been a huge problem for developers up to this point. Consequently, AI has been slow to develop and has not spread widely to improve patient care. Enabling radiologists to develop AI on-premises, at their own institutions, will unlock massively larger data stores available for the development of AI. This will rapidly expand the AI solutions available to us all."[8]

Beyond supporting advancements in diagnostics, AI has a role to play in innovating other aspects of the imaging value chain, including improving the accuracy and consistency of reports, optimizing throughput, improving the value of clinical intelligence, and increasing the overall value of radiology in the patient care continuum.

Reducing imaging errors with AI is an area getting increased attention. The latest data shows that average real-time day-to-day radiology error rates range from 3% to 5%.[9] While that doesn't sound like much, if we take a midrange of a 4% error rate and apply this to the estimated 1 billion radiological studies done each year worldwide, the impact is about 40 million radiologist errors per annum. Other studies show that the retrospective error rate among radiologic studies is as high as 30%.[10]

The use of AI, and specifically machine learning, to consistently recognize patterns within images is one way to call attention to things that might be missed in an image. It comes to the aid of busy radiologists by reducing variation in the number of errors made across populations of radiologists.

Beyond its use for pattern recognition, major imaging vendors are embedding AI into imaging modalities so that technologists can efficiently obtain the right scans in the right manner to answer many clinical questions.

Improving the quality and efficiency of images is being achieved as several major imaging vendors use AI-based positioning systems and image reconstruction to recognize and reduce motion.

Another benefit of AI is in its ability to extend a clinician's knowledge quotient. In the ever-increasing speed to which radiologists and other clinicians must operate, AI not only augments a clinician's diagnostic skills but also helps them fasttrack their clinical knowledge and experience. For example, in the lifetime of their practice, a dermatologist will look at about 12,000 images. An algorithm developed by Google for predicting the presence of skin cancer as initially trained used over 130,000 images.[11]

AI-based solutions are increasingly being used **to improve the efficiency of workflow processes.** In doing so clinicians are able to focus more on high value services. Like other specialties facing increases in clinical workloads and administrative burdens, radiologists are subject to alarming rates of professional burnout caused by inefficient systems and processes.

The application of AI across imaging and other systems is helping to reduce burdens on radiologists by automating processes. This includes systems that prevent referring physicians from placing unnecessary orders, or the use of intelligent protocoling to improve the ability to triage the use of imaging devices and prioritize which scans need to be completed.

The use of speech, vision, and natural language processing capabilities is coming to the rescue in reducing time spent on manual documentation or reentering data into multiple systems. It's also improving a clinician's ability to extract information from other systems such as the Electronic Health Record (EHR) to more easily integrate such information into treatment plans. These same tools are also being used to improve the processes used to generate the "radiology report," which is the foundation for diagnoses, treatment recommendations, and insurance reimbursement.

When it comes to productivity and patient throughput, AI is being used in the registration and scheduling process, especially in outpatient centers, to predict which patients will likely miss their appointments, thereby allowing staff to make extra efforts with these patients to decrease gaps in nonproductive time.

In a broader view, the ability to leverage AI to automate such processes is helping to increase the reach and use of diagnostic imaging.

The Future Role of Radiologists

Radiology has always been one of the top data-driven medical specialties. Historically this has meant mastering the generation and interpretation of vast amounts of unstructured data in the form of images. With AI becoming much more pervasive in health and medicine, radiologists will increasingly be freed from many repetitive or mundane tasks that will be better done by smart machines. This should empower them to go even deeper in applying their expertise in the use of all types of data that contributes to better outcomes and an even deeper role for them to play in the provision of patient care.

Forty years ago, the world saw the first use of full-body magnetic resonance imaging (MRI) machines to generate diagnostic-quality images. As this monumental breakthrough in medicine moved towards becoming mainstream there were pundits that predicted it would lead to the demise of radiologists. In reality the opposite occurred as radiologists leveraged the value of this new technology to help all specialties achieve new heights in quality and outcomes.

When I think about the predictions made about the impact of MRIs on radiologists, and the views of some today on the impact of AI on radiology, I'm reminded of a story of Mark Twain. While in London, a rumor started in the United States that he had taken ill and died. An American newspaper had gone so far as to print Twain's obituary. When presented with a copy Twain's response was, "The reports of my death are greatly exaggerated." This may be a fitting quote for radiologists today.

Notes

1 Ziad Obermeyer, M.D., Ezekiel J. Emanuel, M.D., Ph.D., Predicting the future—big data, machine learning, and clinical medicine, *New England Journal of Medicine*, 2016, www.nejm.org/doi/full/10.1056/NEJMp1606181.

2 AI, Radiology and the Future of Work, *The Economist*, 2018, www.economist. com/leaders/2018/06/07/ai-radiology-and-the-future-of-work.

3 Geoffrey Hinton, Wikipedia, 2019, https://en.wikipedia.org/wiki/Geoffrey_Hinton.

4 Diego Ardila, Atilla P. Kiraly, Sujeeth Bharadwaj, Bokyung Choi, Joshua J. Reicher, Lily Peng, Daniel Tse, Mozziyar Etemadi, Wenxing Ye, Greg Corrado, David P. Naidich, Shravya Shetty, End-to-end lung cancer screening with three-dimensional deep learning on low-dose chest computed tomography, *Nature Medicine*, 2019, www.nature.com/articles/s41591-019-0447-x.

5 Alejandro Rodriguez-Ruiz, Kristina Lång, Stand-alone artificial intelligence for breast cancer detection in mammography: Comparison with 101 radiologists, *Journal of the National Cancer Institute*, 2019, https://academic.oup.com/jnci/advance-article-abstract/doi/10.1093/jnci/djy222/5307077?redirectedFrom=fulltext.

6 Andre Esteva, Brett Kuprel, Dermatologist-level classification of skin cancer with deep neural networks, *Nature*, www.nature.com/articles/nature21056.

7 American College of Radiology Launches ACR AI-LAB™ to Engage Radiologists in AI Model Development, American College of Radiology, 2019, www.acr. org/Media-Center/ACR-News-Releases/2019/American-College-of-Radiology-Launches-ACR-AILAB-to-Engage-Radiologists-in-AI-Model-Development.

8 Ibid.

9 Adrian P. Brady, Error and Discrepancy in Radiology: Inevitable or Avoidable? Insights Imaging, 2017, www.ncbi.nlm.nih.gov/pmc/articles/PMC5265198/.

10 Ibid.

11 Ibid.

Chapter 11

Understanding and Managing the Ethics of AI

What all of us have to do is to make sure we are using AI in a way that is for the benefit of humanity, not to the detriment of humanity.

—Tim Cook
CEO, Apple

Your team has invested an incredible amount of time and effort in developing the first hospital-wide clinical use case using Artificial Intelligence (AI). The focus has been on using AI to reduce unexpected adverse medical events with inpatients. Such events often lead to patients being admitted to the ICU. When this occurs, it is not only a quality of care issue but adds days to their lengths of stay, which becomes a cost issue as well.

In an AI pilot that made use of streaming data and machine learning, your team was able to predict and reduce adverse events by 35%. Plans are now underway to deploy the system across your entire patient population. Your marketing department has done a great job of showcasing this innovation as the top local TV station is setting up in the executive conference room to do a short interview with you.

As you're going through your final briefing before the interview one of the team members responsible for the project provides a breakdown of how the 35% reduction was achieved. While clearly demonstrating an improvement in both quality and efficiency, the 35% reduction in adverse events is a statistical average across all patients included in the pilot. In looking more closely at the statistical average of 35%, you see that the ability to predict and prevent adverse medical events in the pilot was three times more accurate for white males than it was for Hispanic females.

Your assistant comes into your office to say the television crew is set up and ready to interview you on the results of the project…

This simple vignette points out the importance of understanding and managing a new set of issues that are emerging with the use of AI. There are times where AI will clearly provide measurable benefits against your overall goals. At the same time, it can also fall short of principles we hold as important in providing health services. In this case it's an example of safeguarding against prediction bias to ensure that the benefits being seen are applied to all of those served.

When it comes to the legal and ethical considerations of deploying AI, there are new and emerging issues. Such issues go beyond the security and compliance rules and regulations that health organizations must manage within today. In the United States it's the Health Insurance Portability and Accountability Act (HIPAA). In Europe it's the General Data Protection Regulation (GDPR). And while AI is governed by the same laws and regulations as any systems involving Personal Health Information (PHI), there are a number of new issues arising from AI that are currently not addressed by existing laws and regulations.

AI is enabling humans to harness vast amounts of data and make breakthrough advances in medicine and the delivery of health services. This is happening across the continuum of needs, service offerings, and care settings. But as we're already seeing in other industries, advances in the use of AI that bring us daily benefits are also raising a host of questions and concerns. These issues will affect how all goods and services, including healthcare, are provided.

For example, in March of 2019 the world experienced its first fatality with a self-driving car. An Uber test vehicle in autonomous mode struck and killed a 49-year-old pedestrian in Tempe, Arizona.[1] The fatality has been a wakeup call not only for the auto industry but also for many other industries where AI-enabled technologies are being eyed either to augment or outright replace human action and oversight. This event is calling into question many legal and regulatory issues.

With headlines like "The Deadly Recklessness of the Self-Driving Car Industry," it is also giving pause to some who fear reputations are at stake.[2] Innovators in all industries are taking a hard look at the early stage AI research in their fields and at the impact that just one death appears to have had on the level of public trust in autonomous vehicle technology.[3]

In the world of health and medicine it's only a matter of time before an adverse event, including death, will arise due to use or reliance on AI-enabled clinical guidance. In the healthcare sector, stakeholders are redoubling efforts to ensure that ethical principles like those discussed in this chapter are robust and that they safely guide the development of AI-enabled technology in this sector.

From a historical perspective, technology capabilities often get ahead of the lawmakers and regulators in creating standards by which society can best benefit from such breakthroughs. One only needs to look at the advent of the Internet to understand the likely trajectory of legal and ethical issues arising from AI.

In 1998, as the Internet began to go mainstream with consumers and businesses, one would have been hard-pressed to find a full-time "privacy lawyer." This legal discipline began to emerge as issues came forward as governments began assessing and creating privacy laws and regulations to guide and govern the appropriate use of consumer and patient data.[4]

Today, the International Association of Privacy Professionals, or IAPP (founded in 1997), has over 20,000 members in 83 countries. Its meetings take place in large convention centers filled with thousands of people. There's no shortage of topics for IAPP members to discuss, including questions of corporate responsibility and even ethics when it comes to the collection, use, and protection of consumer information.[5]

Just as the Internet gave birth to new public policies and regulations, AI is spawning a new set of issues for governments and regulators and to a new set of ethical considerations in the field of computer science.

Ultimately the question is not only what AI can do. It's what AI should do.

Similarly, will the future give birth to a new legal field called "AI law"? Today AI law feels a lot like privacy law did in 1998. Some existing laws already apply to AI, especially tort and privacy laws, and we're starting to see a few specific new regulations emerge, such as for driverless cars.

But AI law doesn't exist as a distinct field. And we're not yet walking into conferences and meeting people who introduce themselves as "AI lawyers." By 2028, it's safe to assume that the situation will be different. Not only will there be AI lawyers practicing AI law but also these lawyers, and virtually all others, will rely on AI itself to assist them with their practice.

The real question is not whether AI law will emerge, but how it can best come together – and over what time frame. We don't have all the answers, but we're fortunate to work every day with people who are asking the right questions. As they point out, AI technology needs to continue to develop and mature before rules can be crafted to govern it. A consensus then needs to be reached about societal principles and values to govern AI development and use, followed by best practices to live up to them. Then we're likely to be in a better position for governments to create legal and regulatory rules for everyone to follow.

This will take time. Inevitably the advances in technology often occur at a faster rate than regulators and legislators in understanding the use and regulation of such technology. As this occurs it sometimes creates a gray zone for those innovators who are harnessing the power of new technology to do good.

An example of this work is underway by the U.S. Food and Drug Administration (FDA). In a recently published white paper, the FDA recognized that its current approach to the regulation of medical devices – which is based on devices that are static in nature with planned, discrete changes – is ill-suited for "continuous learning" AI algorithms.

For example, under the current framework, changes in an AI algorithm due to exposure to new data from real-world use could trigger additional reviews by the FDA. The consequence would be that whenever the algorithm learns or adapts (which ideally it would with every use), the manufacturer would have to ask FDA to clear (or approve) the algorithm change.

Such scenarios are not likely workable for both medical device manufacturers and the FDA. At the same time, given the current state of AI and of the many challenges associated with continuous learning systems, organizations like the FDA must define rules and processes to adequately protect the public if such use of continuous learning systems is to become mainstream. The FDA is engaging with key constituents to begin a long and challenging discussion intended to find the right balance between new technology, regulatory approaches, and protecting the public.[6]

It is with purpose that we are not covering AI specific to the security and compliance laws and regulations that exist worldwide today. As with any use of personal health information (PHI), AI is governed by these same laws and regulations that health organizations are living up to today.

Instead, the remainder of this chapter outlines five ethical principles that health leaders should be aware of and use. These principles are designed to ensure that those AI systems you develop or deploy from other IT vendors are fair, reliable and safe, private and secure, inclusive, transparent, and accountable. These are adapted from the book "The Future Computed" by Brad Smith and Harry Shum which provides a thoughtful approach to creating a framework for managing AI in an ethical fashion.

The more we build a detailed understanding of these or similar principles – and the more technology developers and users can share best practices to implement them – the better served the world will be as we begin to develop and refine societal rules to govern AI.

Principles

Fairness – AI Systems Should Treat All People Fairly

AI systems should treat everyone in a fair and balanced manner and not affect similarly situated groups of people in different ways. For example, when AI systems provide guidance on medical treatments, it should make recommendations that are accurate for everyone with similar symptoms. If designed properly, AI can help make decisions that are fairer because computers are purely logical and, in theory, are not subject to the conscious and unconscious biases that inevitably influence human decision-making.

And yet, AI systems are designed by human beings, and the systems are trained using data that reflects the imperfect world in which we live. Without careful attention, AI systems can wind up operating unfairly without careful planning due to biases that enters the system. To ensure that fairness is the foundation for solutions using this new technology, it's imperative to understand how bias can be introduced into AI systems and how it can affect AI-based decisions and guidance.

Because AI-driven systems are trained using data that reflects our imperfect world, without proper awareness and control, those systems can actually amplify biases and unfairness that already exist within data sets. They also can "learn" biases through their processing. "Under-representation" in data sets may also hide population differences in disease risk or treatment efficacy.

For example, researchers recently found that cardiomyopathy genetic tests were better able to identify pathogenic variants in white patients than patients of other ethnicities, the latter of which had higher rates of inconclusive results or variants of uncertain significance.

Even data that are representative can still include bias because they reflect the discrepancies and biases of our society. This includes racial, geographic, or economic disparities in accessing healthcare.

Nonrepresentative collection of data also can produce bias. For example, reliance on data collected through user-facing apps and wearables may skew toward socioeconomically advantaged populations. Those who use such devices may have greater access to connected devices and cloud services.

Similarly, genetic testing remains cost prohibitive for many consumers. As such, AI systems that leverage such genetic data sets may be skewed toward more economically advantaged consumers. And data obtained from electronic health records (EHRs) will reflect disparities in the patient populations treated by health systems implementing EHR systems; the uninsured or underinsured, and those without consistent access to quality healthcare (such as some patients in rural areas) often will be underrepresented in EHR data sets. EHR data themselves may introduce bias because they were collected for clinical, administrative, and financial purposes (patient care and billing) rather than for research and, therefore, may be missing critical clinical contextual information.

How can we ensure that AI systems treat everyone fairly? There's almost certainly a lot of learning ahead for all of us in this area, and it will be vital to sustain research and foster robust discussions to share new best practices that emerge.

Reliability – AI Systems Should Perform Reliably and Safely

AI-enabled systems that are deployed in the healthcare sector not only offer great promise but also the potential for injury or even death if they do not operate reliably and safely. In some senses, the healthcare sector has a head start here, in that many of the systems envisioned will be considered medical devices and subject to existing and new regulations.

The complexity of AI technologies has fueled fears that AI systems may cause harm in the face of unforeseen circumstances, or that they can be manipulated to act in harmful ways.

As is true for any technology, trust will ultimately depend on whether AI-based systems can be operated reliably, safely, and consistently – not only under normal circumstances but also in unexpected conditions or when they are under attack.

This begins by demonstrating that systems are designed to operate within a clear set of parameters under expected performance conditions. In all cases there should be a way to verify that they are behaving as intended under actual operating conditions. This means consistently producing the correct or intended results.

Because AI systems are data-driven, how they behave and the variety of conditions they can handle reliably and safely largely reflect the range of situations and circumstances that developers anticipate during design and testing.

For example, an AI system with a vision component designed to assess skin lesions for cancer may have difficulty consistently spotting patterns of concern based on race or skin coloration. This means designers should conduct tests across all skin types. Rigorous testing is essential during system development and deployment to ensure that systems can respond safely to unanticipated situations; do not have unexpected performance failures and do not evolve in ways that are inconsistent with original expectations.

Equally important, because AI should augment and amplify human capabilities, people should play a critical role in making decisions about how and when an AI system is deployed, and whether it's appropriate to continue to use it over time. As noted throughout this book, since AI systems often do not see or understand the bigger societal picture, human judgment is key to identifying potential blind spots and biases in AI systems.

In one example, a system designed to help make decisions about whether to hospitalize patients with pneumonia "learned" that people with asthma have a lower rate of mortality from pneumonia than the general population. This was a surprising result because people with asthma are generally considered to be at greater risk of dying from pneumonia than others.

While the correlation was accurate, the system failed to detect that the primary reason for this lower mortality rate was that asthma patients receive faster and more comprehensive care than other patients because they are at a greater risk. If researchers hadn't noticed that the AI system had drawn a misleading inference, the system might have recommended against hospitalizing people with asthma, an outcome that would have run counter to what the data revealed.[7]

Repeatability is another key factor in ensuring that AI can be relied on in consistently performing across variable environments and situations. One example is a study conducted at the Icahn School of Medicine at Mount Sinai showed that AI tools trained to detect pneumonia on chest X-rays suffered significant decreases in performance when tested on data from outside health systems.[8] Such findings demonstrate the need for AI applications to be carefully tested for performance across a wide range of populations and locations.

These examples highlight the critical role that people, particularly clinicians and those with subject matter expertise, must play in observing and evaluating AI systems as they are developed and deployed.

The dynamic nature of continuous learning AI means we will need to develop new ways to ensure the safety and reliability of such systems. We will need to develop a regulatory regime that ensures that changes a continuous learning system makes to itself, ostensibly improvements, do not instead introduce errors into the model that could injure subsequent patients. But at the same time processes must be created to be more nimble, so as to not require nearly constant revalidation of a medical device using AI.

Privacy and Security – AI Systems Should Be Secure and Respect Privacy

As more of our lives are captured in digital form, the question of how to preserve our privacy and secure our personal data is becoming more important and more complicated. While protecting privacy and security is important to all technology development, recent advances require that we pay even closer attention to these issues to create the levels of trust needed to realize the full benefits of AI.

As we collect an increasing volume of sensitive data about people through an expanding array of devices, we will have to do more to ensure that this data is stored in secure systems. Such systems will be managed by stewards who will be guided by clear rules that protect this sensitive data from improper uses. At the same time, such systems will need to be managed in ways that enable new AI-powered innovations that benefit individual patients and society as a whole.

Simply put, people will not share data about themselves – data that is essential for AI to drive value in healthcare decisions – unless they are confident that their privacy is protected and their data secured. The advances and benefits that AI-enabled technologies will drive in the healthcare sector will not be possible without data governance, and so we must ensure we proceed in ways that build and reinforce patient trust.

These dual objectives of security (ensuring that unauthorized parties cannot access the data) and privacy (ensuring that neither authorized nor unauthorized parties access and use the data for a nonpermitted purpose) are increasingly intertwined with the technology platforms on which the data is captured, stored, processed, and retrieved. The same technology platforms that have resulted in huge strides in AI capabilities are also proving to be the foundation for advances in how we properly manage patient privacy and security expectations.

From a security standpoint, modern cloud platforms enable sensitive data sets to benefit from massive security investments by the companies that build and operate these systems. From a privacy standpoint, these modern cloud systems provide a deep and nuanced set of technical controls that allow data stewards to control access at a granular level as well as to create robust access logs that enable audits to ensure data has not been improperly accessed or used.

Such platforms can replace past practices of shipping large health data sets on portable media, where it can potentially be downloaded by many different parties and onto multiple local servers, with little ability to log or audit access and use. Techniques such as differential privacy and homomorphic encryption provide additional protections, ensuring that sensitive data is less visible and accessible to prying human eyes. Moreover, the machine-based access that these systems enable greatly diminishes the need and opportunity for humans to have "eyes on" review of sensitive data.

Such techniques will reduce the risk of privacy intrusions by AI systems so they can use personal data without accessing or knowing the identities of individuals. It will be critical for AI researchers, policymakers, and even patients to understand the privacy and security promoting advances in technology platforms and how those can be overlaid on law and regulation to result in stronger security and privacy protections for patient data.

Privacy issues associated with patient health information have proven to be some of the more challenging issues. At root, we know that the information contained in a patient's health records can be some of the most sensitive information about a person, and all of us have a strong interest in keeping that information private. But as we move into more complex areas of healthcare research, we also see the emergence of new and more challenging privacy issues.

Research using genetic information has the potential to unleash ever deeper layers of information not just about a patient, but likely also about the patient's distant relatives. Some research projects may also represent a dilemma to a particular patient, raising ethical issues to those patients in tension with an otherwise altruistic sense of sharing personal health data for research purposes that could benefit society.

These nuanced privacy issues will require policymakers and data stewards who are responsible for maintaining and managing patient health information to have a deeper understanding of technology and its interplay with data privacy requirements for patient health data.

In the United States, an Executive Order on Maintaining American Leadership in AI laid out a number of objectives to guide federal agencies' work on AI, including to "foster public trust and confidence in AI technologies and protect civil liberties, privacy, and American values in their application in order to fully realize the potential of AI technologies for the American people."[9]

The Office of the Chief Technology Officer (CTO) in the U.S. Department of Health and Human Services (HHS) has begun to chart a department-wide AI for health strategy to address the objectives set out in the Executive Order, including those related to privacy. As part of that charting process, HHS conducted a series of workshops with experts and stakeholders to gather input during 2019. The first of these workshops held was titled "Sharing and Utilizing Health Data for AI Applications," and a report on that workshop was produced and published by the workshop facilitator.[10]

One consistent theme raised at the first two HHS workshops related to whether the portion of the HIPAA Privacy Rule which establishes the conditions under which protected health information may be used or disclosed by covered entities for research purposes currently provides the right balance, both to protect privacy interests of patients and realize the potential of AI technologies.

An important subset of discussions related to this theme involved how various stakeholders in the healthcare research community interpret key provisions of the HIPAA Privacy Rule and whether advances in technology and the advent of the AI era necessitate additional guidance from policymakers and regulators. The focus of this debate is to ensure HIPAA's provisions are consistently interpreted and applied to promote the twin goals of protecting patient privacy and fostering information sharing to support legitimate research uses of patient data.

Inclusiveness – AI Systems Should Empower Everyone and Engage People

If we are to ensure that AI technologies benefit and empower everyone, they must incorporate and address a broad range of human needs and experiences. Inclusive design practices will help system developers understand and address potential barriers in a product or environment that could unintentionally exclude people. This means that AI systems should be designed to understand the context, needs, and expectations of the people who use them.

AI experiences can have the greatest positive impact when they offer both emotional intelligence and cognitive intelligence, a balance that can improve predictability and comprehension. AI-based personal agents, for example, can exhibit user awareness by confirming and, as necessary, correcting the understanding of the user's intent. Personal agents should provide information and make recommendations in ways that are contextual and expected. They should provide information that helps people understand what inferences the system is making about them. Over time, such successful interactions will increase usage of AI systems and trust in their performance.

Transparency and Accountability

Underlying the principles of reliability, fairness, and security are two fundamental principles: transparency and accountability. Because decisions made by AI health systems will impact patients' health and care, it is particularly important that everyone relying on these systems (healthcare professionals, patients, managed care organizations, regulators) understand how the systems make decisions.

Equally important, as AI health systems play a greater role in both diagnosis and selection of treatment options by healthcare professionals, we will need to work through existing rules around accountability, including liability. As a threshold matter, these systems should provide "holistic" explanations that include contextual information about how the system works and interacts with data.

AI health systems may create unfairness if healthcare professionals do not understand the limitations (including accuracy) of a system or misunderstand the role of the system's output. Even if it is difficult for the users to understand all the nuances of how a particular algorithm functions, healthcare professionals must be able to understand the clinical basis for recommendations generated by AI systems. As discussed above, even where the results of AI systems may be technically reliable, they may not always be clinically relevant to a particular patient. This is the reason why healthcare professionals will need to continue to exercise their judgment between the two.

Transparency is not just how the AI system explains its results. It's also about teaching healthcare providers and users how to interrogate the results. The goal is to ensure that doctors and others relying on these systems understand the limitations of the systems and do not put undue reliance on them.

Recent court cases involving use of algorithms by state officials to assess and revise benefits for citizens with developmental and intellectual disabilities under a state Medicaid program provide a glimpse of how accountability issues will arise and be adjudicated. In these cases, courts required the states to provide patients with information about how the algorithms were created so that patients could challenge their individual benefit allocations.

Beyond transparency, developers of AI-driven health systems should have some degree of accountability on how the systems operate. At the same time there is also accountability amongst those that deploy these systems in medical practice to exercise appropriate judgment when integrating them into medical decision-making. At this point, there remain more questions about how accountability should be addressed than there are answers.

For example, how should the balance of responsibility for use of suggestions provided by AI-driven precision health systems fall between system developers, healthcare institutions implementing the systems, and healthcare professionals utilizing the systems in clinical decision-making? Are healthcare institutions required to independently evaluate each system, and if so, how?

The introduction and use of AI in healthcare continues to evolve. As we look to the future, it's important that we maintain an open and questioning mind on emerging policy and ethical issues while we seek to take advantage of the opportunities and address the challenges that this new technology creates.

Health leaders, policymakers, researchers, academics, and representatives of nongovernmental groups must work together to ensure that AI-based technologies are designed and deployed in a manner that will earn the trust of the people who use them and the individuals whose data is being collected.

Notes

1 www.washingtonpost.com/news/dr-gridlock/wp/2018/03/19/uber-halts-autonomous-vehicle-testing-after-a-pedestrian-is-struck/.
2 https://gizmodo.com/the-deadly-recklessness-of-the-self-driving-car-industr-1831027948.
3 https://medium.com/@baumhedlund/will-the-public-ever-trust-fully-autonomous-cars-3085d81a994.

4 The Future Computed: Artificial Intelligence and its Role in Society, Brad Smith & Harry Shum, Microsoft, 2018, https://news.microsoft.com/futurecomputed/.
5 Ibid.
6 Medical Devices – Artificial Intelligence and Reactions to FDA's Proposed Oversight, The National Law Review, 2019, www.natlawreview.com/printpdf/113024.
7 Can A.I. Be Taught to Explain Itself? Cliff Kuang, *The New York Times Magazine*, 2017, www.nytimes.com/2017/11/21/magazine/can-ai-be-taught-to-explain-itself.html.
8 Artificial Intelligence May Fall Short When Analyzing Data Across Multiple Health Systems, *Science Daily*, 2018, www.sciencedaily.com/releases/2018/11/181109101411.htm.
9 Available at www.whitehouse.gov/presidential-actions/executive-order-maintaining-american-leadership-artificial-intelligence/.
10 Available at www.hhs.gov/sites/default/files/sharing-and-utilizing-health-data-for-ai-applications.pdf.

Chapter 12

The Role of the Cloud in AI

Cloud is about how you do computing, not where you do computing.

—Paul Maritz
Computer Scientist and Software Executive

At the heart of Artificial Intelligence's growing capabilities to fuel the intelligent health revolution is the cloud. And while everyone tends to talk about the cloud, much of what it is and how it drives value is not well understood. This is not to say that health leaders need to be cloud experts to lead health organizations into the world of Intelligent Health Systems. Of the many apps that you use on your smartphone, how many times have you needed to know how they work?

For many reasons, the growing use of AI is based on the "behind the curtain" progress made in the last decade to create secure, industrial-strength cloud services that increasingly power most applications used in our daily lives.

Essentially, cloud computing and AI are partners in that one enables the other. Without cloud computing, current AI capabilities would be quite limited.

And so, why is AI so dependent on the cloud? Simply put, the value proposition of the cloud in driving AI is its ability to enable the collection, storage, and analysis of data at unprecedented scale, speed, and depth.

Coupling this with mobile devices and the ability to connect to information at any time and from any location gives us the ability to reimagine how health organizations attract and serve consumers, improve clinical care processes across care settings and increase the effectiveness of the workforce.

A Bright Cloudy Future

Cloud computing – also known simply as "the cloud" – is a model for enabling ubiquitous, convenient, on-demand network access to a shared pool of configurable computing resources. This includes networks, servers, storage, applications, and services. All of the resources needed or required can be rapidly provisioned and flexibly scaled to meet the changing needs of an organization.[1]

The cloud has many distinguishing features when compared with conventional "on-premises" systems that people have traditionally used to do their computing.[2]

The cloud's system of networked data centers offers users access to immense computing storage capacity. Users access this storage in a scalable fashion, paying for more capacity in times when they require more storage. Think, for example, of a rapidly growing organization that is able to smoothly scale the amount of computer storage it needs to hold its patient and consumer data, without having to continually upgrade its infrastructure as it grows.

In addition to storage capacity, a cloud provider's network of data centers offers users the ability to draw on large amounts of computing capacity, again in a scalable fashion. This is convenient for organizations that experience fluctuations in their computing needs. Think, for example, of clinical research projects involving genomic data that have to rapidly scale up capacity during the research phase but then return to a lower capacity once projects are completed.

It is the cloud's ability to store and process immense amounts of data with huge amounts of computing power that is at the core of data-driven technologies like AI and data analytics.

Due to the distributed and networked nature of the cloud, users can access it anywhere, allowing them to work, record, and access data wherever they happen to be. This is especially valuable in allowing for global reach of any cloud-based services and work that enable areas such as the establishment of global working research communities.

At St Jude Children's Research Hospital in Memphis, Tennessee, researchers and clinicians are advancing the global fight against childhood cancer by combining their collective expertise in research and treatment of pediatric disease, cloud computing, and genomics data analysis to process, store, and share significant amounts of pediatric genomics data.

Since 2010, St Jude has developed and managed one of the world's largest collections of pediatric cancer genomic data. The mission of the research hospital has always been to make the data freely available to researchers, scientists, and clinicians, but technology limitations made providing access to its vast data repositories difficult. By moving the data and genomics program to the cloud, St Jude has expanded its groundbreaking work by allowing researchers worldwide to have access to a half a petabyte of genomics data.[3]

The shift to the cloud among organizations has been rapid. According to Gartner, 89% of companies were using cloud computing in some form by the end of 2016.[4] Many people may be using the cloud today without realizing it. For example, if someone subscribes to online services such as Dropbox, Netflix, Snapchat, Office 365, or Salesforce, they are using a cloud-based service.

The Benefits of AI in the Cloud

AI was once the stuff of science fiction. However, it is now no longer a promise; it is happening now, enriching our personal lives through intelligent assistants such as Cortana, Siri, and Alexa. It is helping hospitals to more easily detect errors by recognizing anomalies in best clinical practices, improving throughput efficiencies in hospitals and a variety of other value-driven use cases.

Such things are possible now because of the computing power and storage made possible by the cloud.

To give a sense of the speed at which cloud-based AI can complete tasks, a system from Microsoft can now translate the entire English-language version of Wikipedia into another major language in less than one-tenth of a second or the time it takes to blink an eye. It has also learned the ability to process human speech to the same level as a human and provide for real-time translation of conversations.[5]

AI's ability to learn and process huge amounts of data because of the cloud offers an immense potential to be used in the development of systems that allow us to improve the quality and efficiencies in providing personalized health and medical services.

Simply put, AI is computational intelligence. As we learned in Chapter 3, AI gives machines the ability to depict or mimic human brain functions including learning, speech, problem-solving, vision, and knowledge generation. The value of this comes when it helps humans complete tasks and make decisions in a quicker and more effective manner. All of this is driven by the advances made in the cloud. Beyond speed and power, here are five other benefits:

Availability of Advanced AI Capabilities: Many AI applications are generally dependent on high-performance environments which include servers with multiple and fast Graphics Processing Units (GPUs). Such systems are expensive and unaffordable for many organizations. AI as a service in the cloud becomes accessible to most organizations at a more affordable price.

Cost-Effectiveness: With computational capabilities and storage always available online, the cloud eliminates the need for expenses for on-site hardware, software licenses, and setup for AI and advanced analytic solutions. It also eliminates the need for on-site data centers and expenses that come with it. From a budgeting perspective, an additional benefit is the shift of expenditures from a capital to an operating expense model.

Increased Productivity: Unlike an on-site server, hard drive, or local storage devices which require IT management, cloud computing is internet based and reduces or eliminates the need for managing activities like hardware setup, software patching, racking, and stacking. Key to productivity gains is in how the use of the cloud frees up valuable IT staff to focus on higher value activities or in how it allows data scientists and informaticists to be more agile in developing or managing AI solutions.

Reliability: Cloud computing solutions typically ensure a higher degree of business continuity. When managing hardware, software, and connectivity in a physically accessible infrastructure the risks of things like crashes and lost files are higher compared with cloud computing. Cloud computing makes things like data backup, disaster recovery, and business continuity easier and less expensive because data can be mirrored at multiple redundant sites on a cloud provider's network.

Rapid Elasticity: This feature of the cloud is especially important for situations where the volume or computing load varies. This means that when demand for computational or transactional services increases you can automatically scale by adding more resources and when demand wanes you can shrink or decrease the resources and costs to fit, thereby not ending up with unneeded resources.

Performance: The large, global cloud computing service providers run on a worldwide network of secure data centers, which are regularly upgraded to the latest generation of fast and efficient computing hardware. This offers several benefits over maintaining a single corporate data center, including reduced latency for applications and greater economies of scale.

On-Demand Self-Service: Most cloud computing services are provided as self-service and on-demand, so that even vast amounts of computing resources can be provisioned on a "just-in-time" basis, typically with just a few mouse clicks, providing health organizations with a lot of flexibility and taking pressure off of capacity planning.

Security: Many cloud providers offer a broad set of policies, technologies, and controls that strengthen your security posture overall, helping to protect your data, apps, and infrastructure from potential threats. This includes specific policies, protocols, and activities to manage data in keeping with security and privacy standards such as the Health Insurance Portability and Accountability Act (HIPAA) (United States) and the General Data Protection Regulation (GDPR) (Europe).

Cloud Computing Delivery Models

There are three core types of cloud service models in use today:

Infrastructure as a Service (IaaS): The provision of processing, storage, networks, and other fundamental computing resources. The customer does not manage or control the underlying cloud infrastructure but has control over the operating systems, storage, and deployed applications. This in effect allows customers to outsource the provision of their core computing functions, utilizing the reliability, scalability, and cost-effectiveness of the cloud.

Platform as a Service (PaaS): This allows the customer to create and deploy custom applications that run in the cloud using programming languages and tools supported by the provider. The customer does not manage or control the underlying cloud infrastructure but has control over the deployed applications.

Software as a Service (SaaS): The provision of "off-the-shelf" applications running on cloud infrastructure. The applications are accessible from any device with an internet connection via a web browser.[6]

Cloud deployment types

The models described above can be deployed in any number of ways depending on the type of service and data used, as well as the level of security required. These include

Public Cloud: As the title suggests, this model is openly available to the general public with data being created and stored on third-party servers. Providers of public cloud services typically offer resources for a low fee or pay-per-use basis and allow users to scale them when required. A private cloud also provides greater opportunities to improve and control overall system performance and scalability.

Private Cloud: A private cloud refers to cloud computing resources used exclusively by a single business or organization. A private cloud can physically be located in a company's on-site data center. Some companies also pay third-party service providers to host a private cloud. From a technical perspective, there is little to no difference between public and private clouds. The main difference is that a private cloud is one in which the services and infrastructure are maintained on a private network. As such, the advantages of a private cloud include greater control over performance and scalability.

Hybrid Cloud: The hybrid deployment model uses a mix of on-premise, private, and third-party public cloud services. This creates a setup where one or many touch-points exist between the environments and gives providers the freedom to choose which apps and resources to keep exclusively in their data center and which to place in the cloud. By allowing data and applications to move between private and public clouds, a hybrid cloud provides organizations with greater flexibility, more deployment options, and helps optimize existing infrastructure, security, and compliance protocols.

Community Cloud: A community cloud deployment model resembles a private one to a large extent; the only difference is the set of users. While a private type implies that only one company owns the server, in the case of a community one, several organizations with similar backgrounds share the infrastructure and related resources.

As the organizations have uniform security, privacy, and performance requirements, this multitenant data center architecture helps companies achieve their business-specific objectives. That is why a community model is particularly suited for organizations that work on joint projects. In that case, a centralized cloud facilitates project development, management, and implementation. Also, the costs are shared across all users.

While the benefits of data and AI in the cloud are clear, it's important to recognize that in real-world health settings there will continue to be dependencies with on-premise data and solutions. Knowing how and when to tie together your cloud and on-premise strategy is key to driving sustainable value.

IT leadership is in the best position to understand how to plan and map data and AI needs the optimal configuration for performance and security. Today's environment typically makes this discussion a moving target that is influenced by factors such as security standards, migration plans for moving applications, and workloads to the cloud and other scenarios that are managed by IT leadership.

The opportunities and challenges of cloud and AI

If the cloud is the engine that underpins the growth of Intelligent Health Systems, the fuel that will power it is data. From AI to machine learning and data analytics, the tools that will generate the insight on which we can build healthier populations are not just data-driven but data-hungry. The more data that these systems can process, the more valuable their outputs, allowing health organizations to improve in providing health and medical services at scale.

Cloud computing represents a seismic shift from traditional computing – not just in what it enables, but in how it is built, managed, and used. To address the risks and threats of the cloud computing era, health organizations will need to adapt existing security programs and policies and enhance current approaches to ensuring the security and resilience of their systems in keeping with existing laws and regulations such as HIPAA and GDPR, but also to new policies and laws being created to address new issues emerging from the use of AI (covered in Chapter 11).

The shift will require not only much closer cooperation with cloud vendors to ensure the security and compliance outcomes required in health but also a change in how the regulatory landscape is managed.

Cloud Computing and AI are partners in the move towards Intelligent Health Systems. With this having already been established, the benefits of these two technologies melding should be obvious to any health organization that wishes to harness the power of this technology. Cloud computing is the engine that drives the value and power of AI. With this pair of technologies constantly reinforcing each other the power and clarity of both your cloud and AI strategies will become exponentially more important in the coming years.

A BRIEF HISTORY OF THE CLOUD – AKA THE INTERGALACTIC COMPUTER NETWORK

When it comes to the evolution of the cloud, much of what we know and use today has its **roots going back to the 1950s.** It started with the emergence of mainframe computing which allowed multiple users to access a centralized computer through "dumb terminals." Providing shared access to a single computer resource was pretty revolutionary at the time.

With the arrival of the 1960s, and in keeping with the times, came some "totally-far-out-ideas" on where shared computing might go. Four years before the TV Series Star Trek debuted, which first popularized the concept of Intergalactic Travel, Dr. Joseph Carl Robnett Licklider (to his friends simply known as "Lick") was imagining and postulating ideas around the creation of what he called an "Intergalactic Computer Network."

Lick was a psychologist and an early computer scientist who, in 1962, put out a series of memos outlining what then was considered science fiction-grade material. At a time when computers were only thought of as mathematical devices for speeding up computations, he wrote about the concept of a global network of time-sharing computers that would include graphical computing and user-friendly interfaces to drive everything from digital libraries to e-commerce.

While serving as director at the U.S. Department of Defense Advanced Research Projects Agency (ARPA), it was Dr. Licklider's persuasive and detailed description of the challenges to establishing a time-sharing network of computers that ultimately led to the creation of the ARPAnet, considered by tech historians as the precursor to the Internet as it was the first network to implement Transmission Control Protocol/Internet Protocols (TCP/IP) protocols. TCP/IP protocols are rules that govern how computer systems communicate in a network that govern how data is transferred from one system to another.

With the 1970s came the concept of virtual machines (VMs). Essentially VMs took the 1950s concept of shared access to a new level by permitting multiple distinct computing capabilities and environments to reside in one physical environment. Virtualization was an important catalyst for the communication and information revolution that was to come in the 1990s.

The 1980s brought about the personal computer revolution upon which cloud computing and shared access would be dependent. This meant there would eventually be devices to connect together. In the late 80s something known as the "Internet" began to come into the public consciousness as a new type of space whereby personal computers could be connected together to communicate and share information. Companies like AOL, Compuserve, and Prodigy began springing up to provide connections and prepackaged services like email. As we rolled into the 90s these top service providers were now offering modem connections that promised an anemic top speed of 9,600 bits per second.

With the 1990s came telecommunication companies that began leveraging virtualization to offer virtual private networks (VPNs). Up until that point, telecommunication companies only offered single dedicated point-to-point data connections. The newly offered virtualized private network connections had the same service quality as their dedicated services at a reduced cost. A VPN extends a private network across a public network, enabling users to send and receive data across shared or public networks as if their computing devices were directly connected to the private network. The use of virtual computers became the starting point for the creation of the cloud's computing infrastructure.

As the story goes, it was 1997 when Professor Ramnath Chellapa gave an identity to this set of things happening between computers operating on public and private networks by defining cloud computing as a new computing paradigm, where the "boundaries of computing would be determined by economic rationale, rather than technical limits alone."[7] In this early stage, this definition of the cloud was used to express the empty space that existed between the end user and the provider.

As we came into the 2000s the rest is history. Salesforce was an early example of using the cloud to deliver software to end users. Amazon introduced and first popularized the use of online retail services and later altered its business model by introducing Amazon Web Services to offer its online services infrastructure to other clients. Microsoft began moving delivery and maintenance of its core software from shrink-wrapped discs to the cloud while curating a host of other cloud-native services.

Notes

1 A Cloud for Social Good, Microsoft, https://news.microsoft.com/cloudforgood/spotlight/what-is-cloud.html.
2 A Cloud for Social Good, Microsoft, https://news.microsoft.com/cloudforgood/spotlight/what-is-cloud.html.
3 St. Jude Children's Research Hospital, Microsoft and DNAnexus Join Forces to Fuel Scientific Discovery, St. Jude Children's Research Hospital, 2018, www.stjude.org/media-resources/news-releases/2018-medicine-science-news/st-jude-microsoft-dnanexus-announce-partnership.html.
4 Ibid.
5 Ibid.
6 Ibid.
7 Keith Foote, A Brief History of Cloud Computing, Dataversity, 2017, www.dataversity.net/brief-history-cloud-computing/.

Chapter 13

Manage Your Data Estate Like Your Finances

> Passion provides purpose, but data drives decisions.
>
> **—Andy Dunn**

Throughout history there's been a diverse and sometimes bizarre set of items used as currency. In Roman times it was salt. In Russia, during the Middle Ages, it was squirrel pelts (claws and snouts were used to make change). At one point in Italy, it was their much-beloved Parmigiano cheese. Whether loyalty points, frequent flyer miles, or baseball cards, currency is nothing more than something a group of people agrees has value.

In today's world of smart-everything, data is becoming a new form of currency used to redefine business models, fuel process change, and drive market success. With this in mind, the question to consider is whether your organization's data estate is being managed with the same care and discipline as your financial assets?

Artificial Intelligence (AI) needs, feeds, and thrives on data. From clinical records to the "digital exhaust" produced by consumers as they complete digital activities, data from all sources are valuable assets used in creating intelligent health services (Figure 13.1).

The good news is that massive amounts of data are available now and growing at an exponential rate in healthcare. For example, the magnitude and explosive growth of medical knowledge and patient information are outpacing the human capacity to keep up and assimilate this intelligence into meaningful form in the daily practices of a clinician. In 1950 a newly minted

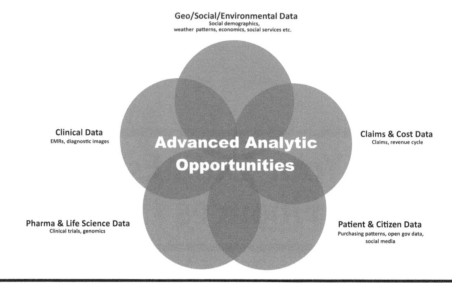

Figure 13.1   All data types from all sources comprise an organization's data estate.

physician going into practice would go 50 years before seeing the body of medical knowledge double. By 2010 medical knowledge was doubling every 3.5 years. Before the end of 2020 it is expected to double every 73 days.[1]

Despite the torrents of valuable data available, many organizations remain behind the curve in harnessing its use. Cross-industry studies show that on average, less than half of an organization's structured data is actively used in making decisions. Even worse is that less than 1% of its unstructured data is analyzed or used at all. More than 70% of employees have access to data they should not. Data breaches are common. Rogue data sets propagate in silos. As the complexity of security and compliance grows, many organization's data technologies or cloud strategies are not up to the demands put on them.[2]

A contributing factor to these issues is that data has traditionally been perceived as just one aspect of technology projects rather than being treated as organizational assets. As a result, the belief has been that traditional application and database planning efforts were sufficient to address the ongoing data issues. In the world of AI and intelligent health they are not.

For AI to create the value necessary to move health organizations forward there must be a recognition and action that treat all data as a strategic asset. Historically, health organizations have used analytics to optimize existing sources of value, rather than leveraging data and analytics to innovate and create new value. Creating new value is what AI is all about. This requires treating data as an asset, just like capital and human resources.

The transition to intelligent solutions is increasing pressure on data and analytics leaders to do more with data assets. In the Gartner 2019 Chief Information Officer (CIO) survey, 45% of respondents reported increasing their investment in data analytics and business intelligence to better support changing business requirements.[3]

Even with the expertise of a Chief Data Officer (CDO), CIO, or Chief Medical Information Officer (CMIO), none of this top talent can be fully effective without a leadership commitment to having the organization become more agile in how it accesses and shares data broadly. This includes the incorporation of outside data sources, while still ensuring that high levels of governance, security, privacy, compliance, and quality are enforced. Balancing the competing requirements of agility and control requires a modern approach to how data is managed. Here are the basic data management building blocks that support the success of your AI strategy.

Creating and Managing Your Data Estate

Successful AI programs that span the needs of an enterprise ride on a solid foundation that is determined by the strength of an organization's data estate. Simply put, a data estate refers to all the data your organization owns, controls, manages or uses regardless of where it is stored. The goal of migrating this data to the cloud or modernizing your environment on-premises is to make it easier and faster to gain important insights to fuel innovation. A modern data environment allows you to empower employees, engage customers, optimize operations, and transform products on a repeatable basis and at scale.

The massive growth in data, and the increasing need for everyone to get immediate insights, demand fast and highly scalable data platforms. When cloud, data, and AI work together, they offer new opportunities for people and organizations to innovate, grow, and achieve more than ever before. The healthcare industry is changing the way it interacts with patients through the use of the cloud, data, and AI to enhance self-care through connected medical devices. The industry is moving to data modernization by analyzing data to offer personalized patient care often, resulting in reduced operational costs. This growth of data is driving the need for data modernization.

Data modernization refers to the process of restructuring how data is collected, stored, and managed to take advantage of new technologies.

Events such as software end-of-support and data center consolidation can be opportunities to modernize a business's approach to data management.

Anyone that has ever been in the trenches knows that working with real-world data is messy. It often spans various data and media types. It changes constantly and often includes valuable knowledge that is not readily usable.

In most cases, the amount of time and energy spent on things like data discovery and preparation actually exceeds the time spent on analytics and getting to actionable insights. As noted below, a recent study by IDC suggests that 80% of your data specialist's time goes toward getting ready with only 20% of their time being spent deriving value from the data (Figure 13.2).[4]

While the "plumbing" aspects of data management are not as sexy as creating predictive models, getting your data estate in order is foundational to the success of any enterprise-wide AI strategy. Here are several areas to consider in your move to becoming a data-enabled organization.

Data Unification: One of the most valuable benefits of unifying data is to create a single view of a patient or consumer. Such efforts lay the foundation to perform many types of behavioral analytics. This includes having a more holistic view of an individual patient for care planning or in the ability to create an aggregated view to assess a population of patients within a service area.

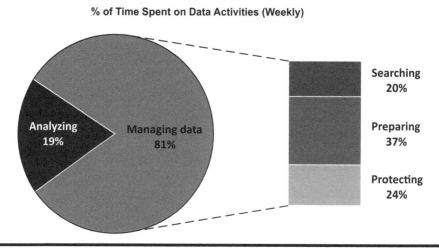

% of Time Spent on Data Activities (Weekly)

Analyzing 19%

Managing data 81%

Searching 20%

Preparing 37%

Protecting 24%

Figure 13.2   How many hours per week on average do you spend on each of the following data-related activities? (IDC's Data Integration and Integrity End-User Survey, November 2017.)

Interoperability: Data unification is highly dependent on data interoperability. This relates to the creation of a standard health information technology infrastructure that allows for the seamless electronic access, exchange, and use of health information.

For example, the chart below lists data sets used by a major health system to power three machine learning use cases: predicting inpatient flow, Rx variation, and chronic obstructive pulmonary disease (COPD) progression. While such data exists in most health organizations, the challenge for data scientists and others is the effort required to provision, stage, and shape it into a usable format to provide predictive intelligence that can be automated and incorporated into ongoing clinical workstreams (Figure 13.3).

While progress is being made, true interoperability remains fragmented and uneven according to a recent report from the Office of the National Coordinator for Health Information Technology's (ONC) Health Information Technology Advisory Committee (HITAC) notes.[5]

Data	Patient Flow — Inpatient Flow	Utilization & Cost — Inpatient Rx Variation	Pop Health & Disease Mgmt. — COPD Disease Progression
Patient Demographics	✓	✓	✓
Diagnosis Info	✓	✓	✓
Orders/Results	✓	✓	✓
Medications	✓	✓	✓
Problem lists	✓	✓	✓
Vitals	✓		✓
Allergies		✓	
Social Determinants of Health (SDOH)	✓	✓	✓
Provider Information	✓	✓	✓
Facility	✓	✓	✓
Insurance	✓	✓	✓
Claims - Post adjudicated			✓
Claims - Transactions			
Wearables & IOT			
Encounter Details	✓	✓	✓

Figure 13.3   Data sources used to power machine learning use cases (KenSci).

The latest efforts to improve interoperability include use of Fast Healthcare Interoperability Resources (FHIR®, pronounced "fire") as a standard framework that leverages the latest web standards and applies a tight focus on implementation. For patients and providers, its versatility is being applied to mobile devices, web-based applications, cloud communications, and Electronic Health Record (EHR) data sharing using modular components.

As interoperability standards and cloud-based solutions improve, government entities such as The U.S. Department of Health and Human Services (HHS) are working to propose new rules to support seamless and secure access, exchange, and use of electronic health information. The goal of such efforts is providing patients and clinicians with the access they need to all of a patient's health information, helping them in making better choices about care and treatment.

Finally, an area that is growing in importance is the acquisition, management, and use external data that, when added or combined with the traditional health and medical data typically generated and used by health organizations, adds greater depth and fidelity to the predictive capabilities of AI in health.

For example, data on social determinants of health (SDH) is increasingly being incorporated into AI initiatives in health. SDH are the **conditions in which people are born, grow, work, live, and age**, and the wider set of forces and systems shaping the conditions of daily life.[6] These forces and systems include economic policies and systems, development agendas, social norms that may be causal factors in health inequities, and health status of people that should be factored into AI programs to better manage the health of individuals and populations of people.

Real-Time Insights Delivery: Most traditional analytical initiatives in health organizations have been focused on old data and processes that summarize what happened in the past. This is akin to looking in the rear-view mirror. The process tells you where you've been but doesn't necessarily help you understand how to get to your destination. There is an increasing ability, especially with cloud-based solutions, to aggregate and present data and information in near real time, thus allowing greater opportunity for rapid understanding and response. And with the help of machine learning we can extend the intelligence process from looking at what just happened to predicting what will occur in the future.

Knowledge Mining: An organized data estate provides the opportunity to retrieve information and extract insights within a vast amount of data. A variety of powerful intelligent tools enable knowledge mining by using built-in AI capabilities to uncover latent insights from all your content – documents, images and media, including the ability to discover patterns and relationships in your content, understand sentiment, extract key phrases, and more.

Data Governance

Data governance is a set of processes that ensure that data assets are formally managed throughout the enterprise so that data can be trusted and that people can be made accountable for adverse events that happen because of low data quality. It's the management of the availability, usability, integrity, and security of your organization's data assets.[7] The key focus areas of data governance include availability, usability, consistency, data integrity, and security.

While all health organizations have staffing expertise as well as policies and monitoring activities for privacy and security, many do not have an organizational-wide data governance program so that data is managed in a way to maximize its value against clinical and operational goals.

One study focusing on the role and importance of data governance notes that the single greatest challenge to the success of data governance programs is the difficulty in identifying its costs and benefits.[8]

Today, best practice data governance programs include a governing body, and this body works to set standards, refine procedures, and creates accountability for all data assets.

The Data Governance Committee should practice a cultural philosophy that believes in governing data to the least extent necessary to achieve the greatest common good. Quite often, organizations will either overapply data governance in their enthusiasm for the new function; or underapply data governance due to their lack of experience. The best approach is to start off with a broad vision and framework, but limited application, and expand the governance function as needed.

Like a finance committee, a data governance committee should be a subcommittee of an existing governance structure, with the oversight responsibility to influence and make changes to workflows, resolve data quality conflicts, and develop complex data acquisition strategies to support the strategic clinical and financial optimization of the organization.

Increasingly, health organizations are enlisting the expertise of Data Stewards who are knowledgeable about the collection of data in the source transaction systems such as the EHRs, cost accounting, scheduling, registration, and material management systems. Data stewards are integral to the mission of a data governance committee as their role is to ensure that data governance processes are followed, guidelines enforced, and that recommendations for improvements to data governance processes are brought forward for action.

Creating a Data Culture

A well-curated data estate will only create value if it's used by those responsible for the ongoing activities of the enterprise.

As data volumes increase, the importance of an enterprise data culture grows. To promote an enterprise "value of data" culture, organizations often need to make behavioral, cultural, and operational improvements.

A data-driven culture within an organization is created by leaders that recognize and promote data as a critical business asset to empower clinicians and staff by providing them with knowledge and tools to allow them to access and turn data into actionable insights and impactful intelligence.

In creating and executing an AI strategy, some organizations focus on building a team of data scientists and top data talent to advance their goals. On their own, such teams are capable of developing and deploying AI capabilities within the organization, but such efforts will have higher failure rates if the organization has not created an enterprise-wide culture that embraces and uses data.

Creating a data-driven culture is a balancing act that not only requires the approval and advocacy of top leaders but also the acceptance and adoption by frontline staff. This requires ongoing communications and engagement with stakeholders to help them understand and believe that the culture you're trying to foster will further empower them in their own work.

A data-driven culture begins by putting those business users in the driver's seat, and furnishing them with the tools to quickly and easily extract meaningful insights from data.

Good governance, good data, and great results

AI initiatives often start with great optimism but end with less-than-satisfactory results. A key predictor of success almost always is the condition of the data estate on which any projects are built.

Health organizations that are serious about AI can no longer afford to treat data management as anything less than what it is – the linchpin for making intelligent health real and practical. Organizations seeking to thrive in the intelligent health world will connect the "data dots" through investments in staffing, expertise, and systems so that their data is accurate, complete, and consistent to empower people and processes in doing more.

AI initiatives often start with great optimism but end with less-than-satisfactory results. A key predictor of success almost always is the condition of the data estate on which any projects are built.

Health organizations that are serious about AI can no longer afford to treat data management as anything less than what it is – the linchpin for making intelligent health real and practical. Organizations seeking to thrive in the intelligent health world will connect the "data dots" through investments in staffing, expertise, and systems so that their data is accurate, complete, and consistent to empower people and processes in doing more.

Notes

1 Peter Densen, MD, Challenges and opportunities facing medical education, *Transactions of the American Clinical and Climatological Association*, 2011: 122: 48–58.
2 Leandro DalleMule, Thomas H. Davenport, What's your data strategy? *Harvard Business Review*, 2017, https://hbr.org/2017/05/whats-your-data-strategy.
3 The 2019 CIO Agenda: Securing a New Foundation for Digital Business, Gartner, 2019, www.gartner.com/document/code/366991?ref=grbody&ref val=3920433.
4 Stewart Bond, Data Intelligence in Context: Enabling Data Governance for Digital Transformation, IDC Technology Spotlight, 2018, http://idcdocserv.com/us44514218.
5 Annual report Workgroup Update, Office of the National Coordinator of Health Information Technology Health Information Technology Advisory Committee, 2019, www.healthit.gov/sites/default/files/facas/2019-02-20_HITAC_AnnualReport_WG_Presentation.pdf.

6 About Social Determinants of Health, World Health Organization, 2017, www.who.int/social_determinants/sdh_definition/en/.

7 James Gaston, A Recipe for Analytics, Key Ingredient #3-Data Governance, HIMSS Analytics, 2018, www.himssanalytics.org/news/analytics-key-ingredient-data-governance.

8 The Future of Enterprise Information Governance, The Economist Intelligent Unit, 2008, http://graphics.eiu.com/files/ad_pdfs/EMC_InfoGovernence.pdf.

Chapter 14

The Importance of Intelligent HIT Vendors

> The number one benefit of information technology is that it empowers people to do what they want to do.

—**Steve Balmer**

Best known for his book *Crossing the Chasm*, Geoffrey Moore is an organizational theorist who has a knack for simplifying complex topics in the business world.

A while ago Moore simplified the world of information technology (IT) by famously dividing all IT systems into two camps – Systems of Record and Systems of Engagement.

The thinking goes like this: Systems of Record are the primary systems of an organization designed to handle clinical and business transactions. These are essentially our data repositories. There are fundamental Systems of Record in health organizations, including for patients (Electronic Health Records [EHR]), staff (Human Resource Information System [HRIS]), and the assets of the organization (Enterprise Resource Planning [ERP], Financials).

Systems of Engagement are interfaces that sit on top of Systems of Record. They allow users to share information found in these systems and collaborate on mission critical activities. Examples include secure email and instant messaging, voice apps, enterprise platforms for data integration, collaboration, and comprehensive analytics that are compliant with mandated security protocols.

With the advent of Artificial Intelligence (AI), the world of enterprise software is beginning to experience an identity crisis. There is a new addition coming to be known as Systems of Intelligence (SOI). The disruptive nature of SOI is that it's a new layer in the overall IT stack. Its purpose is to enhance the value of Systems of Record by using data from multiple sources. The goal of this is to generate previously unseen insights or improved functionality through the use of AI (Figure 14.1).

SOI are impacting all types of enterprise software because it couples the breakthroughs in the use of data and machine intelligence with a framework for how additional value is created by these systems. Let's use Electronic Health Records (EHRs) as an example of the change that's coming (and perhaps already underway).

The adoption and use of EHRs is now ubiquitous across the healthcare industry. As a key system of record its purpose has been to serve a static digital repository for historical information on patients and consumers.

In moving from paper to digital recordkeeping the benefits are EHRs have included better ability to exchange health information electronically, greater up-to-date accuracy of information at the point of care, improved collaboration, and enhanced privacy and security.

And while these and other benefits have improved the way health and medical services are provided, EHRs have not necessarily transformed the care process for two reasons.

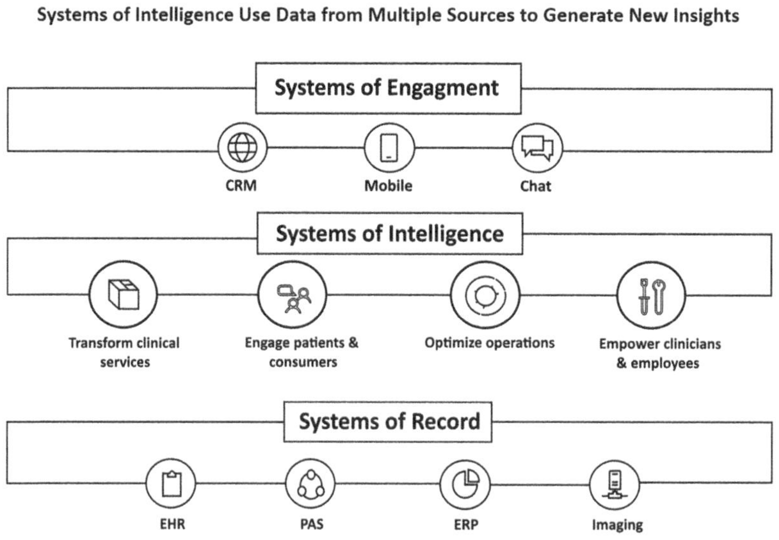

Figure 14.1 Systems of intelligence utilize data from other systems to generate previously unseen insights.

First, digitizing information previously stored on paper is akin to freezing water. The form was changed but the underlying elements remained the same. Changing its form made data more retrievable and secure, but the overall process remained essentially the same in how clinicians use data to assess a patient's situation, make a diagnosis, and recommend treatment options.

Second, while EHR systems contribute to improved patient care and outcomes, the use of these systems remains a point of contention among some clinicians due to issues that sometimes overshadow the benefits. These include usability and an increased administrative burden, which can be contributory factors in the growing issue of physician burnout.

A study by the American Medical Association (AMA) highlights the challenge of digitizing data without changing or improving the process used by clinicians to use Systems of Record. In examining how physicians spend their time the study notes that providers spend about 27% of their total working time interacting face-to-face with patients. In contrast they spend 49.2% of their time doing EHR or deskwork. Additionally, physicians also spend an average of two hours working on EHR data entry outside of their office hours.[1]

When looking at the potential for extending the value of EHRs through SOI there are various ways to increase the value derived from the data while improving the clinician's experience. The focus of such efforts is to use AI to make interactions with EHRs more customized and personalized. A few examples include:

■ Helping providers assemble and package the components of clinical documentation to more efficiently create notes that accurately reflect a patient encounter or diagnosis.

■ Intelligently assimilating and aggregating data streams from home monitors, wearables, and bedside medical devices, which when combined with other EHR data, can feed predictive analytics algorithms or help autopopulate notes with vital signs or records of changes in health metrics.

■ Intelligent interfaces: AI can also be used to improve the usability of EHRs by automating the experience each clinician has based on their specialty, current patient or case mix, use patterns, and preferences. Additionally the use of "suggestive analytics" on a just-in-time basis will make clinicians aware of relevant clinical information and best practice protocols based on smart systems recognizing patterns across data that a human on their own may not see.

Going beyond the current role of automating the collection, storage, and retrieval of information, EHRs will be capable of generating valuable insights on an individual patient or across a population of patients.

And whether stored in an EHR or elsewhere, AI will create data bridges to extend the ability of clinicians to more easily leverage data and content from all systems used in the care process. The combination of EHRs and genomic data is one example for AI going forward.

Like the health clients they serve, most software and IT system vendors are early in their AI journeys. The ones that will be market leaders will be first in understanding and deploying AI in their solutions in service of improving clinical and business outcomes.

Going forward, the introduction of intelligent solutions in health organizations will come in two ways.

First, as the AI in health market is in its early stages, many activities and solutions are currently being driven by staff and consultants who extract data from an organization's Systems of Record to then develop predictive capabilities. This approach works but is normally independent and external to the current role of Systems of Record. Additionally, there are a growing number of vendors that specialize in providing single-threaded solutions that deliver value. These normally focus on a specific range of use cases (often referred to as Narrow AI).

Second, as the market evolves and matures, major Systems of Record vendors will become leaders in the Intelligent Health System market as they embed AI directly into their products and solutions. As this occurs the future of your Intelligent Health System strategy will become increasingly more dependent on selecting and using vendors whose products and roadmaps are aligned to your needs and expectations. To this end, it is important to understand a vendor's current AI capabilities as well as their AI roadmap.

Beyond understanding their strategy and roadmap to make their solutions more intelligent, it's important to define and make known your expectations for how such systems will support your goals. In this regard there are certain actions that can be taken to ensure your investment in major systems going forward that contribute to your effectiveness. These include

■ Creating a charter that defines your organization's view on the role and use of AI in transforming clinical and operational workflow to be more efficient and consumer-centric. This charter document can be used to define and promote your go-forward expectations with current and future vendors providing IT solutions.

- Defining AI criteria and vendor expectations for inclusion in Requests for Information (RFIs) and Requests for Proposals (RFPs) when considering any new purchasing or licensing agreements. This should include methods of delivery and management of future AI-driven solutions including whether cloud, on-premise or hybrid, and the rationale for which model is being used.
- Developing an assessment methodology to be used internally and with vendors to test and demonstrate that AI capabilities are not only secure and compliant but assessed to ensure that they are being ethically applied. This means defining the minimum requirements that are used to safeguard against the introduction of bias, ensure transparency, and address other factors relating to the ethical use of AI (covered in Chapter 11).

The emergence and use of SOI will create some demanding and complex information management challenges for Health Information Technology (HIT) vendors and the clients they serve. The current reality is that the HIT vendor market is at varying stages of technology maturity with the introduction and use of AI. The speed to which this evolves will be directly related to the needs and expectations of the market. As this occurs, having your organization's voice heard will serve to expedite vendors in making their offerings more intelligent and supportive of your success.

With the above in mind, here's a sampling of how a select group of HIT vendors are using AI today with a view to what is coming in the future.

Epic: Seth Hain, Vice President for R&D for Analytics and Machine Learning

Epic is a leader in developing software for healthcare organizations around the world in support of its mission of helping people get well, helping people stay well, and helping future generations be healthier.

Its EHR is used across care settings including hospitals, clinics, retail health locations, skilled nursing facilities, hospice, and in-home. Today over 250 million citizens from around the globe have a health record in Epic.

Seth Hain is Epic's Vice President of R&D for Analytics and Machine Learning. In this role, he works with healthcare leaders to understand client needs. He guides the use of data and analytics to provide insights at the point of care in order to improve outcomes for patients.

"The emergence of artificial intelligence in healthcare provides new opportunities to address key challenges faced by our clients," says Hain. "In the inpatient space it's enabling clinicians to better manage traditional risks and improve quality from the moment a patient walks in the door until they are discharged. Examples of this include applying machine learning to predict falls, deterioration, and readmissions. With the shift to value-based care and a more holistic approach to understanding and managing the needs of patients, we're focusing AI on how to better manage chronic disease and proactively identify high-risk patients."

While many IT vendors are in the aspirational or planning phases for making their solutions more intelligent, Epic has already invested in developing its Cognitive Computing Platform. The capabilities of the platform are already being adopted at scale. In 1 year alone, Epic users leveraged it to make more than 5.1 billion predictions. Beyond these numbers, which show interest and rapid uptake, the results of clients using its predictive capabilities are driving measurable improvements in care, including

- North Oaks Health System in Hammond, LA reduced its sepsis mortality rate by 17.7% and decreased codes outside of the ICU by 40%.
- Lee Health in Fort Meyers, FL reduced its 7-day readmission rate by 35%, saving nearly $750,000 in a 6-month period.
- Rush University Medical Center in Chicago, IL reduced the number of patients who left the Emergency Department without being seen by 50%, improving patient care, and increasing the annual revenue by $750,000.

Epic's cognitive computing capabilities are enhanced with the use of cloud services, which improve the accuracy of the models in the Epic library by allowing them to be localized to an organization's patient population. With the benefit of the cloud providing scalable computing power, users get real-time predictions without taking a performance hit to on-site production databases.

The Cognitive Computing Platform includes a model library that serves as a starter set for many organizations focusing on

Acute Care: This includes improving outcomes by predicting things like in-hospital falls, patient deterioration, and readmissions. Other areas include monitoring ICU outcomes with models that benchmark ICU lengths of stay and in-hospital mortality.

Operations: Predictive capabilities in this category focus on areas like estimating and managing inpatient census, calculating remaining length of stay, and determining the risk that a patient will be a no-show for an appointment.

Population Health: This area focuses on helping care managers intervene to keep patients healthy with models that predict events such as a patient being hospitalized or having an ED visit, abusing opioids, or developing hypertension.

Workflow: Machine learning is being used to improve workflows behind the scenes by learning from patterns in users' behavior to provide a personalized, easier-to-use system.

In addition to using prebuilt models within the library developed by Epic, clients can use the same tools for Epic-released models to develop and deploy their own custom or third-party algorithms. The use of cloud services gives those developing their own predictive models access to tools it enables to develop their own predictive models that enable developers to rapidly test and deploy them into production.

"While helping clinicians better manage quality and outcomes is always top of mind, the ongoing challenge is how we use data and predictions to improve all operational aspects of the care process," says Hain. "In this regard, we're focused on two areas. The first is how AI can be applied in an integrated fashion to create efficiencies in areas like billing, operational throughput, and staffing. The second part of this is in how we're using AI to help people get the most out of their workflow. This means using AI to help staff have the right information that is efficiently provided at the right time so that the focus is always on the patient. We refer to this as relevance within our software."

Hain also notes that part of both the opportunity and challenge of using AI to create Intelligent Health Systems is getting clinical leaders to rethink clinical care processes based on the new capabilities AI provides.

"A key factor in successfully deploying AI is looking at how we manage things differently," says Hain." For example, if we look at the way in which outreach is done for a population of diabetics, the typical process is to prioritize outreach based on a single variable such as A1c test results. We know that so much more goes into the long-term management of this important population than a single measure. We have the capability today to synthesize hundreds of variables already being captured in various systems that when we add them up provide a much deeper understanding of each individual patient as well as the characteristics of the entire population. That's the power AI."

Looking forward, Hain sees other important trends unfolding today that impact the future development and value of cognitive services, including.

Greater inclusion and use of data on social determinants of health (SDOH). SDOH are the **conditions in which people are born, grow, work, live, and age,** and the wider set of forces and systems shaping the conditions of daily life.[2] These include economic policies and systems, development agendas, social norms that may be causal factors in health inequities, and health status of people that should be factored into AI programs to better manage the health of individuals and populations of people.

An abundance of such data exists and is readily available from government and private sources. Incorporating such data into an organization's data estate for use with clinical data is a key element driving AI systems that have deeper impact.

Use of an intelligent data infrastructure. While there are many organizations running AI and machine learning pilots today, the data platform used in the future must be able to efficiently move new predictive models from pilot into full production. This means being able to embed predictive models that work in real time into the normal workflows that are utilizing the latest data. The goal of such an infrastructure is to make intelligence actionable through tactical tools and applications such as the creation and use of intelligent patient lists and dashboards or by using predictive models to improve clinical decision support.

Monitoring and managing all predictive models that have been deployed. An area taking on greater importance as predictive capabilities become more mainstream is the systemic monitoring of all algorithms to ensure that they are used in keeping with an organization's clinical, regulatory, and ethical standards. How predictive models perform varies based on many factors such as data itself or the environment in which predictive models operate. For example, the use of a deployed predictive model for clinical decision support might be affected by the addition of new hospitals whose data is added as part of a merger or acquisition. Another example is where a predictive value may demonstrate overall effectiveness in improving performance but have wide variance in effectiveness based on variables such as age, gender, and race. Systems that automatically monitor and safeguard such inconsistencies are critical to the success of AI being deployed at scale.

Becton Dickinson medication management: Ranjeet Banerjee, President

BD (Becton, Dickinson and Company) is one of the largest medical technology companies in the world, whose mission is "advancing the world of health" by improving medical discovery, diagnostics, and the delivery of care.

As worldwide president of BD's Medication Management Solutions business, Ranjeet Banerjee spends a lot of time thinking about how to make the management and distribution of drugs better. "As simple as it sounds, getting the right medication to the right patient at the right time and right cost across the care continuum is a very complex process involving thousands of variables. While automation has been in place for some time within the medication management space, there remain a lot of very manual activities creating inefficiencies at the individual level for the nurses, doctors and pharmacists as they deliver care as well as systemic quality and cost challenges at a macro level."

With prescription drug expenditures topping $360 billion worldwide there's lots of room for improvement.[3] For example, a survey on *Medication Management and Safety* notes that more than 75% of physicians, nurses and pharmacists surveyed describe current medication management processes as "flawed," "fragmented," "disjointed," and "primitive."[4]

BD sees the use of advanced integrated analytics, in combination with their connected devices, as an integral element of a holistic solution that can address key healthcare challenges. As such, BD is prioritizing the development and use of AI across their continuum of medication and infusion solutions.

"The use of artificial intelligence in every phase of medication management provides the opportunity to make it safer, simpler, and smarter. I see AI being applied to improve performance and outcomes for patient safety, medication availability, and clinician productivity," says Banerjee.

There are a number of examples where BD is harnessing data and analytics to deliver better outcomes in the medication management process.

To drive process improvements in the infusion space, smart infusion pumps can communicate with the pharmacy to monitor the status of the IV solution bag and alert the pharmacy when a bag will run dry. By automating this process there is better adherence to medication use while lowering the staff time required to monitor and manage infusion pumps. Another area of benefit with smart infusion pumps is the ability to program infusion pumps directly from the EHR rather than having to have humans manually programming each pump. This benefits staff in greatly reducing the amount of time spent on this repetitive activity.

AI is improving system efficiencies through intelligent inventory control, which takes advantage of AI to provide advanced decision support to pharmacy staff to optimally managing medication inventories across an organization. This works by using machine learning and other analytical tools to evaluate current patient needs, dispensing trends, and historical restock data to then predict optimal inventory needs for each patient care area. Upon human review and approval recommendations made by the system are then automatically made.

A third area in which BD is leveraging AI is to better manage drug diversion – the misappropriation of opioids or other drugs by healthcare workers. A workflow-based application, supported by machine learning algorithms, helps hospitals identify anomalous behavior (similar to credit card fraud detection) by healthcare professionals who could benefit from retraining on best practices or who actually suffer from a substance abuse disorder and need help. This supports clinicians in need, improves the safety of patients, and limits a hospital's liability.

Siemens Healthineers: Thomas Friese, Senior Vice President for Data Architecture & Technology Platforms

With its origin dating back to 1847, Siemens Healthineers has seen and been a big part of the changing landscape in health and medicine for 173 years. With 45,000 employees in over 75 countries its mission today is to enable healthcare providers worldwide to increase value by empowering them on their journey towards expanding precision medicine, transforming care delivery, improving patient experience, and digitalizing healthcare.

And while the Siemens Healthineers solutions footprint is diverse across laboratory diagnostics and therapy solutions, it is best known for its work in the area of diagnostic imaging. On an average, its devices touch 240,000 people every hour of the day.

When it comes to the road ahead for Siemens Healthineers, the role and impact of data and AI is central to its future and a core part of its go-forward solutions strategy.

"There are significant changes affecting the healthcare provider market including increasing cost pressures, consolidation, and the ongoing quest for improving quality and outcomes," says Thomas Friese, senior vice president for Data Architecture & Technology Platforms. "At the same time, we are seeing a profound technological paradigm shift that is being driven by digitalization and the application of artificial intelligence which we see as a core part of our strategy going forward."

Today, Digital Data and AI is one of five priorities defined in the Siemens Healthineers Strategy 2025 and seen as an anchor to precision medicine, future therapies, and optimizing the patient's journey.

"Our goal is to leverage data and AI to provide more people with access to efficient, effective, affordable healthcare services," says Friese. "There are a number of areas where we are applying AI now against this goal that focuses on unwanted variation and optimizing clinical and operational workflows for our clients."

A seemingly simple but important example is the use of AI to improve the process of image acquisition, which impacts the cost and quality of performing a CT or MRI scan. Siemens is augmenting the skills of the imaging tech by applying deep learning algorithms to placement images from a stereoscopic camera that recognizes a patient's geometry and physiology to automatically determine optimal patient placement when a scan is being completed. The results include increasing image quality while decreasing the time and variance that occurs without the use of AI.

"The interpretation phase of the imaging process is another area that holds promise for the use of AI. Because of the increasing capabilities to intelligently process and interpret greater quantities of data the reading process will change for radiologists. We are even moving towards Magnetic Resonance Fingerprinting (MRF) which allows clinicians to skip the image and instead work directly towards diagnosis with the raw data," says Friese.

MRF uses quantitative information to generate a more precise understanding of a patient's condition. MRF data could increase objective comparisons in follow-up studies by using reliable, absolute numbers. Ultimately, aided by AI, quantitative measurements will likely lead to more personalized treatments. MRF is at the frontier of a new dimension in quantitative imaging.

Siemens also sees the use of narrow AI algorithms as a means of supporting clinicians in their daily practice. Studies show that there is a correlation between diagnostic errors and a physician's workload. The use of AI to assist clinicians in important but repetitive processes, such as the segmentation of anatomical structures or lesions, or the standard classification of images is a good example of its current capabilities to reduce unwarranted variation as well as the cognitive burden faced by physicians.

"We further see applications of AI algorithms – often times imaging based – make a difference during treatment today, especially when fusion of multi-modal data (e.g., angiography and ultrasound during a cardiac intervention) is required. A lot of assistive functions are implemented into the treatment guidance systems of today to again lower to cognitive burden of the physician performing a procedure to help them navigate and use the vast amount of data available to them," says Friese.

Going forward with the increasing capability to tackle basic image interpretation tasks automatically, Siemens will be able to generate more structured data describing what is present in the unstructured images of today, with less manual labor involved. This higher amount of structured data enables new applications focusing on intelligent workflow guidance and clinical decision support to become more pervasive in everyday practice. Gradually the available data for an individual patient or even a bigger cohort or population will turn into machine-understandable data that enables new applications of AI.

Notes

1 Physician EHR Use, Workload Trumping Face Time with Patients, Sarah Heath, EHR Intelligence, 2016, https://ehrintelligence.com/news/physician-ehr-use-workload-trumping-face-time-with-patients.
2 About Social Determinants of Health, World Health Organization, 2017, www.who.int/social_determinants/sdh_definition/en/.
3 Prescription Drug Expenditure in the United States from 1960 to 2019 (in Billion U.S. Dollars), Statista, 2019, www.statista.com/statistics/184914/prescription-drug-expenditures-in-the-us-since-1960/.
4 Medication Management and Safety Study: Professionals, Patients Cite Progress, Concerns, HIMSS Analytics, 2017, https://go.bd.com/rs/565-YXD-236/images/Medication%20Management%20Study.pdf.

Chapter 15

From Aspiration to Execution

There is no instant pudding.

—Dr. W. Edwards Deming
on the matter of transformation

Most health leaders understand that Artificial Intelligence (AI) has the power to change how health services are provided. What many don't know is how to transition from deploying a few pilots to delivering transformational AI at scale. Moving from aspiration to execution is where many organizations flounder in having their investment of time and money produce the payoffs that are promised with AI.

A survey of more than 1,100 executives by Accenture Strategy quantifies this dynamic. Results showed that companies know that AI is a critical piece of their competitive strategy moving forward. At the same time less than half (45%) say they have deployed fully sustainable AI programs that are delivering benefits as planned. More than half of all organizations (53%) were still in pilot mode or in the early stages of adoption.[1] Overcoming this "deployment gap" to drive sustainable value at scale happens when the issues and conditions noted in this book are understood and addressed as part of a cohesive and coordinated strategy.

The difference between AI leaders and laggards often comes down to the strength of an organization's AI strategy that defines the goals and deliverables and provides an operational roadmap to achieve these goals. In developing an enterprise-wide AI plan here are six things to pay attention to.

Complete an AI Reality Check

No matter how far along you believe your organization is in its AI journey, it's important to have a clear and realistic view of your starting position. Completing an assessment should go beyond an inventory of AI pilots and projects underway. Instead you should evaluate critical aspects of your readiness to execute by addressing the following questions:

■ What interactions with consumers, patients, and your own staff provide the best opportunities to use AI to improve quality, consumer satisfaction or efficiencies?

■ Is it clear how existing and new AI projects will measurably support your mission and goals? What are the metrics you will use to measure value and success?

■ How will AI be used to differentiate your organization in the market and reduce the risk of losing out to a competitor?

■ What is the condition of your data estate to be able to efficiently curate new initiatives?

■ Are clinicians and staff aware of your organization's aspirations and planning efforts in how AI will be used? Are they supportive or resistive to the changes likely to occur as AI becomes more pervasive in the organization?

■ Are your organization's culture and decision-making processes oriented towards being data-driven or data-resistant?

■ What is the status of your "top talent" on which planning and execution will be dependent? Key roles can include (but are not limited to) your Chief Technology Officer (CTO), Chief Information Officer (CIO), Chief Data Officer, Chief Medical Officer (CMO), Chief Security and Compliance Officer (CISO), Clinical Informaticists, and Chief Human Resource Officer. Important: Execution of an enterprise-wide AI initiative does not require the presence of all of the positions noted above (especially in smaller organizations). Instead it's important to have staff capable of managing the various components of an initiative.

■ Beyond compliance with privacy and security standards, is your organization's use of AI being evaluated to ensure it is done in keeping with the ethical standards and of values of the organization?

Creating a snapshot of what is occurring in your organization today provides leadership with a starting view of organizational attitude and skills, technology infrastructure, process improvement opportunities, and general level of readiness on which to build.

Lay a Solid AI Foundation: People + Data

Your organization's ability to successfully plan and launch an enterprise-wide AI program that supports your move to becoming an Intelligent Health System will be built on a foundation that includes the following cornerstones:

Enterprise AI Is a Team Sport: Early AI initiatives in health organizations often begin with AI specialists and IT leaders who are early adopters. Such efforts are important but often struggle and fail to gain broad traction. At the same time AI initiatives bubbling up from the clinical or business side of the organization often fail because they have limited focus and don't take full advantage of the data and IT talent required to successfully drive and sustain such projects. Simply put, the success of AI pilots can be done with a small group of motivated, like-minded team members but the success of a sustainable, enterprise-wide AI program cannot.

As noted throughout this book, the success of AI across your organization is highly dependent on empowering a team of diverse stakeholders to plan and execute your AI strategy. This requires the inclusion of people representing clinicians, IT, AI and data specialists, business process owners, HR, security and compliance, marketing, and consumer experience.

Once you define a team to drive planning and implementation of your AI strategy it's important to define and communicate an organizational operating structure that enables this group to lead efforts within the organization. Some organizations create a planning and operational steering committee. Others may add AI responsibilities to existing departments or divisions (e.g., Office of Chief Digital Officer or automation group). Increasingly, health organizations are establishing AI Centers of Excellence (CoE) to build a foundation and give added visibility to AI efforts. Some organizations are also establishing stronger lines of accountability for AI initiatives by creating board committees specifically related to AI.

Whatever form is given to the team chosen, there should be a clear charter established that defines its role and responsibilities. Typical responsibilities for this group include education and advocacy within and outside the organization, identification and prioritization of use cases, and development of policies for governance and accountability.

Finally, the AI team should create and manage a digital platform for collaboration, support, and resource management. Think of it as the one-stop shop for AI efforts: a virtual environment where business and tech professionals will share resources (such as data sets, methodologies, and reusable components) and collaborate on initiatives.

Data Is the Currency for AI – Be Ready to Spend It: All AI initiatives start with great optimism but many end with less-than-satisfactory results. A key predictor of success almost always is the condition of the data estate on which projects are built and maintained. As noted in Chapter 13, AI runs on data and has an almost endless appetite. This includes having data available in the right format at the right time to initially create and train algorithms and applications.

Equally important is the recognition that AI must be integrated into technologies and workflows that operate around the clock. This means that these algorithms and applications usually require a continuous flow of new data to learn and perform.

As you begin developing your AI strategy you can increase both the success and "time to value" of initial AI projects by engaging early with your data and IT leaders to understand and invest as needed, in connecting the "data dots" that AI requires, including an evaluation of your staffing, inhouse expertise, and systems. The ultimate goal is to ensure that the data needed to support your AI projects is accurate, complete, and consistent.

Nix Moonshots in Favor of Well-Curated Use Cases

Imagine being a Saturday morning jogger and in a moment of excitement deciding to sign up to run a full marathon the following weekend. Such is the case with some health leaders who get so excited about the possibilities with AI that they commit to initial projects that are unrealistic in scope or complexity.

While somewhat harsh, Oracle's co-CEO summarizes the danger of moonshots: "Without execution, 'vision' is just another word for hallucination."

Leaders should recognize and champion that AI is going to transform the way people work and the way services are provided. In doing this it's important to think big but start with well-defined opportunities that have a high probability of success against your clinical or operational goals.

Initial projects should be selected on the basis of each opportunity's potential value, cost, and speed of delivery. Once you've locked in on which projects to pursue, treat them as "test and learn" opportunities. In doing so, each project undertaken helps create an operational framework that can then be used as the launchpad for future projects and use cases. Done right, selecting and pursuing an AI use case for one specific task can both enhance an existing process or solve a well-defined business problem, while simultaneously creating the potential to scale what you learn to other parts of the enterprise.

Recognize that every new IT initiative that your organization takes on creates risk. AI projects are no different. When selecting initial AI projects, a variable that determines risk is the level of complexity of the scenario or use case you choose to take on. One way of "derisking" early projects is to evaluate the complexity of the use case. In this regard there are several components of project complexity to be considered, including

Technical: What is the level of technical complexity for a given project? In addition to traditional hardware/software considerations this includes determination of computing model (cloud, on-prem, or edge) as well as which approach to be used for developing and managing the "intelligent" component of the project (type of algorithm or AI component plus method for developing/delivering/maintaining).

Data: Data complexity includes type of data (structured/unstructured), availability (does it exist? location, integration and interoperability), security and compliance considerations (data required to predict and reduce claims denials may have different compliance requirements than data needed to predict clinical outcomes).

People and Processes: How many people are involved in a process that will be changed as a result of an AI initiative? What level of effort will be required to revamp the set of activities, interactions, and hand-offs that occur within the old or existing process to be improved by the introduction of AI? Breaking down processes into six sigma-like elements uncovers ways in which AI can add value while also identifying just how much change will be required to realize its value.

Recognize that different use cases have different types and levels of complexity. A high-value project may be low in data and technical complexity but of very high complexity when it comes to the number of people whose work will have to change in order to realize the intended value of a project. The goal is to use such criteria to select projects that match the organization's initial readiness and then enable the organization to increase the complexity of projects undertaken over time.

Expect imperfection in your initial efforts and use early projects to identify areas for improvement. The dual benefit of initial projects should be to deliver measurable value against your goals while defining what the organization needs to do to be better in creating a repeatable process for future projects.

Understand and Manage Workforce Impact

The very nature by which AI creates value (automation and augmentation) will at some level impact every clinician and employee who is part of your organization. And whether real or exaggerated, many of these people have concerns about the ways in which AI will affect their work, practice, and career. AI often creates stress for staff and, over time, requires the organization to plan for large-scale retraining. Think about a nurse working alongside a virtual nursing assist or a call center employee taking over the interaction of a chatbot.

Engaging early in exploring AI and its impact on the future of work provides the opportunity to evaluate what changes you should be prepared to make. It also helps to bring your people along in a way that makes them more likely to be more supportive as change occurs. While some jobs may eventually be eliminated through AI automation, most jobs will be improved or enhanced as AI will take over many repetitive and time-consuming tasks.

AI will influence the structure of how work is done. From the time initial AI pilots begin, smart organizations invest early in planning and education activities to increase the capacity of their people to adapt and change with the times.

Focus on Delivering Secure and Responsible AI

As we covered in Chapter 11, the AI legal and policy landscape is in its infancy worldwide. Health leaders, policymakers, and legislators are working to ensure that AI-based technologies are designed and deployed in ways that will earn the trust of the people who use them. As this occurs it is important to recognize that laws and regulations governing AI in health will continue to evolve as its use becomes more pervasive.

Most countries are revising existing laws and regulations that govern general protections for security and data privacy in the healthcare world to reflect the changing nature and use of this data. New initiatives are also popping up in various countries to address privacy, data sovereignty, and ethical issues specific to algorithms and other aspects of AI.

In developing your AI strategy, it will be imperative to have systems in place to stay abreast of the legal and regulatory changes that are occurring. For example, in the United States health organizations are all used to managing all data classified as Personal Health Information (PHI). In 2018 Europe's General Data Protection Regulation (GDPR) went live creating sweeping changes in how data must be managed. As of this writing the California Consumer Privacy Act (CCPA) is set to go live. A close examination of GDPR and CCPA shows that they have differences but both give consumers the right to see and control how organizations collect and use their personal data while providing additional recourse, should they incur damages due to bias or security breaches.

Beyond complying with the laws and regulations specific to your geography, there are situations when AI can help an organization achieve measurable success in clinical and operational improvement in keeping with existing laws and regulations but still miss the mark when it comes to addressing key ethical principles such as fairness and transparency.

This means that your AI strategy should take into account the current and evolving laws, regulations, and ethical standards that will govern your actions and ensure that your efforts are safe and trustworthy.

The top resources for managing this part of a plan include your Chief Security and Compliance Officer, Compliance Team, inhouse or external legal counsel, and the Chief Data and Information Officer.

Become Your Organization's AI CEO (Chief Evangelist Officer)

An important factor in driving cultural change in support of your AI strategy is having employees and other key constituents understand what is happening and why it is their interest. Leaders who are committed to successfully developing and deploying the organization's AI strategy are usually the most persuasive evangelists in educating and influencing key people to embrace the changes necessary for the strategy to succeed.

Ideally, ever member of the team appointed to plan and execute your organization's AI strategy will become a Chief Evangelist Officer. The role includes articulating the vision set forth in the plan, soliciting input and involvement, countering misperceptions and changing the mindset of employees to lower the fear factor, and increase the excitement factor for what is ahead.

In this regard an important role of leaders is to be effective storytellers. While professional communications staff (HR, PR, marketing) can support the packaging and positioning of change, organizational leaders must be on the frontlines to effectively communicate the "what and why" messages surrounding transformation. Telling that kind of story about the future is not a one-time event. Leaders should be consistent and persistent in bringing the core message home to all. Additionally, the message being delivered should be tailored to fit with the many internal constituents found within the organization.

Measuring Success

The creation and execution of an AI strategy is a multiyear event and, in some ways, a continuous process that never ends. Whether it's at the launch of your strategy or a review several years down the road, it's important to develop and measure your success against specific goals. In broad terms here are the three areas around which specific key performance indicators should be developed.[2]

New growth. How successful has your organization been in creating new services, solutions, and business models? This can be gauged by assessing the percent of revenue outside historical core services that can be attributed to new growth.

Core repositioning. How effectively has the company adapted its legacy business to change and disruption? Internally this can be gauged by evaluating volume and key performance indicators (KPIs) pre- and post change. Externally this can be measured by evaluating the retention and growth of specific patient populations, increases in market penetration both geographically (increasing volumes from core service area or generating increased volumes in new geographies) and demographically (attracting higher volumes of millennials other target audiences).

Financial performance. How have the organization's growth, operating expenses, gross, and net revenue changed compared to previous operating periods or as compared to relevant industry benchmarks during the transformation period?

AI Leaders and Laggards

Today most health leaders recognize the potential of AI and are doing something with it. The question is not whether something is being done but rather what is being done. More important to measurable success is how you will curate and manage your investment to get the results you want to compete and thrive in the emerging world of intelligent health. In this regard, and as time moves on, there will be AI leaders and laggards.

AI leaders will be characterized as those who mobilized to embrace the changes AI will bring about even in the face of the uncertainties of the currently emerging market.

They will be known to have enlisted a select group of clinicians and staff to lead an organizational transformation effort that benefits and empowers all staff in playing to the highest side of their expertise and capabilities. It will include using the power of AI to reimagine and redevelop the patient and consumer journey to provide more personal experiences.

AI leaders will set out clear goals for AI and use early projects to support these goals. They will create a continuous learning cycle that benefits future projects and builds momentum internally that becomes a competitive advantage externally. They will leverage the value of their data as a true asset that can be monetized in service of the organization's general mission and specific goals.

AI laggards will likely be those that adopt a "wait and see" attitude while moving at traditional speeds for the industry. They will spend too much time within the safety of their "pilot period" while trying to figure out which way the market is moving. AI will mainly be treated as another technology initiative with goals mainly tied to making existing processes incrementally more efficient rather than reimagining and reinventing how work will be done differently.

Data will mainly be treated as a byproduct of existing activities and mainly used to look at what happened rather than what is to come. Clinicians and staff will be left wondering about their future in light of what they see and hear about the impact of AI on how they will work or whether they will even have a job.

The Choice Is Yours

What role will AI ultimately play in the future of health and medicine? No one really knows the exact form it will take, but all indications are that it will be both disruptive and transformational.

In the end AI is a tool. Whether it's a hammer or a heuristic analytics engine, the value of any tool comes from the skills and intended purpose of the user whose hands it's in. For those who choose to use its power wisely, AI will make health organizations and practitioners smarter, processes more efficient, experiences more personalized, and consumers more satisfied.

We are witnessing a new shift in computing. It's a move away from static systems and towards a mobile-first and AI-first world. It is forcing us to reimagine a new order in the health world that allows us to create a more natural, seamless way of interacting and caring for those served by healthcare.

AI in health is a new journey for all of us. And like any new journey, the initial steps you take will be some of the most important when it comes to where this journey will take in your career and ultimately in your ability to be a force for change.

Notes

1 Andrew Sinclair, Jeffery Brashear, John Shacklady, AI-The Momentum Mindset, Accenture Strategy, 2018, www.accenture.com/us-en/insights/strategy/ai-the-momentum-mindset.
2 Scott D. Anthony, Evan I. Schwartz, What the Best Transformational Leaders Do, *Harvard Business Review*, 2017, https://hbr.org/2017/05/what-the-best-transformational-leaders-do.

Chapter 16

The Road Ahead for AI

> I believe AI and its benefits have no borders. Whether a break-through occurs in Silicon Valley, Beijing, or anywhere else, it has the potential to make everyone's life better for the entire world.
>
> **—Fei-Fei Li**
> *Codirector of Stanford University's Human-Centered AI Institute*

The great French author Margeurite Duras once wrote: "the book doesn't really end. As it closes, it is just a beginning." And while this book was not written to provide a precise map for the future of Artificial Intelligence (AI), it hopefully provides a current look at the state of AI in health and how to jump start your own move towards Intelligent Health Systems. Where AI in health, and in the rest of our lives, is going over the long term is anyone's guess.

In 1985, the prediction of a young Bill Gates that someday there would be a personal computer in every home was met with quite a few snickers from the tech titans of the day. In 1995, it was hard to imagine how pervasive the Internet would become in everyone's life. Amazon was a river in South America. In 2005 twitter was something birds did. In 2007 most people didn't imagine that the cell phone would eventually function as something other than a device to talk to other people.

And so, with the evolution and use of AI, what will become ordinary in the coming decade is hard to imagine today. Predicting where AI will take us in the future is much like predicting where a tornado will land. We may know it's coming but can't really know where it will land until it happens.

We can take some comfort in the fact that Stanford and other universities have joined together to take on the task of completing a One Hundred Year

Study on AI. Launched in 2014, the initiative is a long-term investigation of the field of AI and its influences on people, their communities, and society. It considers the science, engineering, and deployment of AI-enabled computing systems. As its core activity, the Standing Committee that oversees the One Hundred Year Study forms a Study Panel every 5 years to assess the current state of AI.[1]

Just as the early stages of other major tech trends eventually impacted the world in profound ways, there will be many experiments and discoveries in using AI. In health the greatest opportunity is in our ability to harness the power of our growing stockpiles of data to improve the delivery of health and medical services. Some of these efforts will fail while others will make initial headway only to become niche solutions. A few will positively change the world of health delivery at scale. The trick is to know which ideas will be transformational in the years ahead.

AI is already rewiring our views on healthcare delivery. When it comes to the next few years, there are already certain areas where we can expect use of AI to drive significant change and value. According to an analysis by Accenture, key clinical health AI applications in the United States alone can potentially create $150 billion in annual savings by 2026. The assessment defined the impact of each application, likelihood of adoption, and value to the health economy.

The top three applications that represent the greatest near-term value include robot-assisted surgery ($40 billion), virtual nursing assistants ($20 billion), and administrative workflow assistance ($18 billion). As these and other AI applications gain more experience in the field, their ability to learn and act will continually lead to improvements in precision, efficiency, and outcomes (Figure 16.1).[2]

Beyond such analysis of which use cases will drive the most value are a host of areas and ideas that are in the early stages of being explored and pursued. There is an almost endless number of ideas being tried to utilize AI to improve our approach and results in health and medicine. Here are a few worth considering.

Precision Medicine

What if, at some point in the future, every baby got a DNA report card at birth that would risk rate and offer predictions about their chances developing diabetes or cancer or their risk of developing addictions to things like

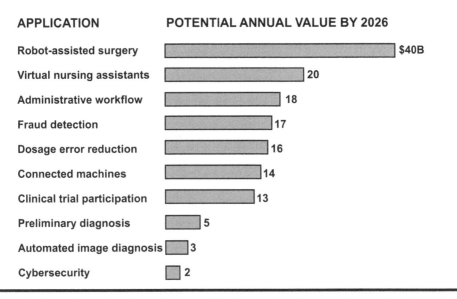

APPLICATION | POTENTIAL ANNUAL VALUE BY 2026

Robot-assisted surgery — $40B
Virtual nursing assistants — 20
Administrative workflow — 18
Fraud detection — 17
Dosage error reduction — 16
Connected machines — 14
Clinical trial participation — 13
Preliminary diagnosis — 5
Automated image diagnosis — 3
Cybersecurity — 2

Figure 16.1   Ten AI applications that could change health care (Accenture).

tobacco, alcohol, or opioids? Having such a "life map" would not only allow us to personalize health and medical services down to the individual level but also bring forward a host of other ethical considerations.

As the National Institutes of Health (NIH) puts it, Precision Medicine is "an emerging approach for disease treatment and prevention that takes into account individual variability in genes, environment, and lifestyle for each person."[3] This approach will allow doctors and researchers to predict more accurately which treatment and prevention strategies for a particular disease will work in which groups of people. This is in contrast to a historical one-size-fits-all approach, in which disease treatment and prevention strategies are developed for the average person, with less consideration for the differences between individuals.

Based on this definition, AI will be at the center of any medical solutions that are able to personalize health and medical services down to the level of each patient and consumer. Precision medicine will be driven by AI to not just identify the right treatment for a particular patient but also individualize all aspects of healthcare for that patient, including disease risk and prognosis prediction. This will lead to better disease detection and prevention.

To be able to ponder all those individual variations, medical professionals have to gather incredible amounts of information and have the ability to analyze, store, normalize, or trace that data. On their own, humans are not capable of managing all of these variables. This is where AI comes into the picture.

In the foreseeable future AI will support the true practice of precision medicine in intelligent health organizations by being deployed to analyze big medical data sets, draw conclusions, find new correlations based on patterns found in the data that are specific to an individual patient. This will support a doctor's ability to develop and decide on care pathways that are specific to each patient.

For maximum impact, AI algorithms will also be used by clinicians to consider the latest academic research evidence and regulatory guidelines before recommending personalized treatment pathways to high-risk, high-cost patient populations. AI will also be used to expedite the process of clinical trial eligibility assessment and generate plans that suggest evidence-based drugs.

With these current and future capabilities that are AI-enabled come a host of benefits and risks. On one hand such capabilities can be used to have women at high risk for breast cancer get more mammograms and those at low risk got fewer which would allow us to catch more real cancers and set off fewer false alarms.

At the same time, the predictive capabilities of AI are never 100% perfect. Will consumers and society really want to know who *might* develop Alzheimer's or an Opioid addiction? What if someone with a low risk score for cancer puts off being screened only to develop cancer anyway?

It is for such reasons that those driving towards making precision medicine mainstream with the use of "genetic fortune-telling" are proceeding with caution. Or as behavioral geneticist Eric Turkheimer puts it, the chance that precision medicine will be used for both good and bad is what makes it "simultaneously exciting and alarming."[4]

A Quantum Leap for Health

While quantum computing is heavily hyped it should not be ignored as it holds great promise in a technology paradigm shift that most people simply can't imagine.

Quantum computing is a type of nonclassical computing based on the quantum state of subatomic particles. Quantum computing is fundamentally different from classic computers, which operate using binary bits. This means the bits are either 0 or 1, true or false, positive or negative. However, in quantum computing, the bit is referred to as a quantum bit or qubit. Unlike the strictly binary bits of classic computing, qubits can, strangely, represent a range of values in one qubit. This representation is called "superpositioning."[5]

In case that definition lost you, imagine your laptop having the combined powers of every superhero in the Justice League. Quantum Computing would open the door to increased computing powers that would move us from taking years to solve complex data problems to hours. Its application to everything from cancer research to drug development would be immense. Things such as DNA gene sequencing could be performed in seconds instead of hours or weeks.

Gartner predicts that by 2023, 20% of organizations will be budgeting for quantum computing projects, compared to less than 1% today and suggest that any real-world benefits are at least 5 years out.[6]

Emotional AI

Imagine a time in the not-to-distant future when your personal device will know more about your emotional state than your friends or family. The ever-improving components of AI that allow machines to identify or predict what humans are feeling are giving rise to what is now being called artificial emotional intelligence or Emotional AI. This is where machines can detect emotions from multiple channels like voice, facial recognition, email, and texts just the way humans do… maybe even better.

Today, innovative retailers are putting AI-enabled technology in their stores to evaluate the sentiment and emotional state of shoppers. In the future, this information will likely be used to have in-store displays change to match the state of mind of shoppers.

When it comes to consumer and patient feedback, emotional signals can provide valuable insights based on changes in facial expressions, tone and pitch of voice, body language, and even neurophysiological activity conveyed through biometric markers that could automatically be built into the care process.

In the world of health, there are many potential applications for emotional AI, including the ability to help clinicians diagnose and treat diseases such as depression and dementia. It also provides an opportunity for consumers to self-monitor and manage their own physical health emotional well-being. For example, at a recent Consumer Electronics Show (CES), appliance companies were already showcasing smart refrigerators that interpret how you feel, which might help those trying to lose weight or change their diets.

Intelligent Testing

Related to the Precision Medicine movement will be the rise of intelligent testing which leverages machine learning and genetic data to improve the diagnostic capabilities of general testing.

An early example of this is Adaptive Biotechnologies which is working to decode the human immune system. It focuses on how data from the immune system can in the future be used to diagnose and treat diseases and has figured out a way to genetically sequence T-cell and B-cell receptors, the main players of the body's adaptive immune system. Sequencing the genome of these receptors is difficult, because, unlike the rest of the human genome, these genes rearrange over time.

In using machine learning and AI to crack the code to the human immune system, Adaptive is working on a diagnostic tool that could one day allow doctors to detect diseases early with a single blood test. Ultimately such intelligent tests would be part of an "immunoscreen" included in a routine checkup to detect diseases as well as improve treatment recommendations based on the precise nature of understanding the situation of an individual patient.

Today, one in ten babies are born prematurely. What if there were a simple blood test that could predict if a pregnant woman is at risk of giving birth prematurely based on small amounts of genetic material that floats "cell-free" in an expectant mom's blood? [7] Such work is already underway as it's now easier to detect and sequence the small amounts of cell-free genetic material in the blood and then use the growing predictive capabilities of AI to identify women likely to deliver prematurely which then gives physicians advance warning and allow them to take measures to reduce the likelihood of delivering early, thereby increasing the chances of both survival and the delivery of a healthy baby.[8]

Biohacking

Move over Steve Austin as bionic humans may be coming (for younger readers Steve Austin was the main character in a 1970s TV series, "The Six Million Dollar Man," who was instilled with bionic capabilities).

Biohacking refers to the application of IT hacks to biological systems – most prominently, the human body. While there are many sci-fi like ideas that make their way around the internet, future options for health and medicine range from simple diagnostics to deep neural implants. For example, biochips hold the possibility of detecting or predicting diseases from cancer to smallpox before the patient even develops symptoms. Such chips would be made from an array of smart molecular sensors that can analyze biological elements and chemicals.

We've already seen early examples of biohacking making their way into mainstream medicine. The Food and Drug Administration (FDA) gave approval recently for use of the world's first "artificial pancreas," which continuously monitors and measures glucose levels for those with Type 1 diabetes and then automatically delivers the appropriate dose of insulin.[9] Today there are more than 283 million people who must manage their Type 1 diabetes. This intelligent, closed-loop system will provide diabetics with greater freedom to live their lives without having to consistently and manually measure glucose levels and administer insulin.

In the United Kingdom a woman recently was the recipient of what may be the world's first in-heart microcomputer which is designed to improve the care of those with heart failure. The wireless device allows clinicians to track patients in real time and predict when a patient is approaching a situation that requires medical attention or intervention. In the United Kingdom, heart failure is the number one reason for hospital admissions. Researchers believe that in the future such technology can improve the health of patients while reducing hospital admissions by 40% and saving the National Health Service (NHS) 75 million pounds annually.[10]

Obviously there are many legal, ethical, and societal questions that arise from biohacking, but increasingly the technology and AI capabilities will bring this to the forefront of medicine in the not-too-distant future.

The Advent of Data Whisperers

Among the data science and informaticist communities are those who believe that within large data sets are undiscovered patterns that, if known, would be invaluable in the diagnosis and treatment of diseases and medical conditions. Essentially the view is that the data we possess is constantly "whispering" valuable things to us that we either aren't paying attention to or do not currently have the tools to hear what the data is telling us.

An example of this is the work of two Microsoft scientists, and a Columbia University graduate student published a study in *The Journal of Oncology Practice*. The article explains how, by analyzing very large numbers of general queries on Microsoft's search engine Bing, they were able to identify people who have pancreatic cancer, even before they had been diagnosed with the disease.[11]

Pancreatic cancer has extremely low survival rates – just 3% of pancreatic cancer patients live longer than 5 years. Their research indicates that this kind of early detection might double that rate.[12] They still have a long way to go before their research makes its way into common medical practice, but it offers a preview of how the ability to look at large amounts of data through the right AI technology-assisted lens can uncover potentially lifesaving information that was previously impossible to detect.

Unifying Mind and Machine with Brain–Computer Interfaces

Using computers to communicate is not a new idea by any means, but creating direct interfaces between technology and the human mind is a cutting-edge area of research that has significant applications in health and medicine.

Brain–computer interfaces (BCIs), backed by AI, acquire brain signals, analyze them, and translate them into commands that are relayed to output devices that carry out desired actions.[13] The main goal of BCI is to replace or restore useful functions to people disabled by neuromuscular disorders such as cerebral palsy, stroke, or spinal cord injury.

Until recently, the dream of being able to control one's environment through thoughts had been in the realm of science fiction. However, the advance of technology has brought a new reality. Today, humans can use the electrical signals from brain activity to interact with, influence, or change their environments. The emerging field of BCI technology may allow individuals unable to speak and/or use their limbs to once again communicate or operate assistive devices for walking and manipulating objects.

The goal of many BCI projects is to access as many neurons as possible because that would give scientists more precise reads on activity that underpins walking, speech, and mood, among other brain functions. They can then turn neural recordings into electrical signals that can be fed into a robotic device or back into the nervous system to produce movement or vision to help patients, according to experts.

New technologies are being developed that blur the lines between computers and biology. The emerging field of neurotechnology involves brain–machine interfaces, neuroprosthetics, neurostimulation, and implantable devices that not only augment nervous system activity but expand its capabilities.

Most notable among the various academic organizations and companies pursuing BCIs is Neuralink. Founded by Elon Musk the company is working towards the introduction of a therapeutic device and platform that would eventually be used to treat neurological conditions and be safe enough to turn the implantation surgery into an elective, outpatient procedure.[14]

Creating an Intelligent Data Collaboration Graph of Medicine

The inherent nature and benefits of a secure, global cloud infrastructure, combined with the ever-increasing power of intelligent data-mining and extraction tools are leading some on the pursuit of creating a unified knowledge repository. The goal is to intelligently connect all major data systems together for the purpose of a megaknowledge base to be used to help manage the health of individuals and populations.

In the next few years medical AI systems that have been deployed will have learned from their past experiences based on patient data, physician responses, treatment outcomes, and a variety of other information. Democratization of AI will likely become more commonplace with new data models emerging that allow health organizations to collaborate and collectively learn from each other.

An early example of this can be found in the work of the American College of Radiology (ACR) that recently developed the ACR AI-LAB™. This initiative provides a data science toolkit and platform designed to democratize AI by empowering radiologists to develop algorithms at their own institutions, using their own patient data, to meet their own clinical needs. The idea is to allow any participating organization to develop high quality algorithms that address local clinical needs while also providing options for such algorithms to be shared.[15]

Augmented Reality

Simply put, Augmented Reality (AR) is the process of putting digital images on top of a user's surroundings. In doing this, AR technology enhances the surrounding environment by overlaying digitally generated images on various surfaces around a user which can be used to bridge the gap between reality and imagination. And while it's often related to its own category in the tech world it is fully dependent and driven by many components of AI.

The use of AR will evolve, but currently is in use to assist surgeons in providing simulations and ancillary information on demand as well as enhancing training by providing highly interactive experiences.

Conversational AI

As noted in Chapter 3, intelligent voice capabilities have now reached parity with the skill levels of humans in the ability to speak, listen, and comprehend conversations. Add a dose of medical intelligence to natural language capabilities with a healthy dose of compliance constructs and you enable an AI-powered, personalized conversational healthcare experience that can scale across all experiences between consumers, providers, and payers.

Today, many organizations are moving in the direction of using conversational AI to leverage and extend information and services currently provided by humans. In the United Kingdom, the NHS is already rolling out conversational AI to help citizens diagnose and understand their health problems. The program allows citizens to receive NHS-verified health information by using simple voice commands which empower people to take more control of their own care while reducing pressure on hospitals and clinicians.[16]

Going forward conversational AI will be increasingly enhanced with the addition and integration of knowledge management capabilities. Combining this with deep learning to help bots improve responses for every single interaction will allow for context-based replies through Natural Language Generation that will make it increasingly hard to differentiate the smart machines and smart clinicians.

As this occurs the application of conversational AI will become more common and pervasive in its uses, including automation through clinical assistance, companions for seniors living alone, new parents in need of "just-in-time" guidance, and a variety of on-demand uses by clinicians in operating theaters and procedure rooms.

Making Global Health Smarter

In the coming decade, the growing footprint of the cloud plus the burgeoning capabilities of AI will drive game-changing improvements for underserved communities in global health. Most impacted by this tech revolution will be the reduction or elimination of historical barriers to provide health and medical services to remote areas in low and middle-income countries (LMIC).

AI will become increasingly pervasive in its application to improve access to health and medical services. One example of its application is in addressing shortages of trained healthcare providers, including ultrasound technicians and radiologists, which can significantly limit access to life-saving care in developing nations around the world.

When it comes to improving access to needed services for expectant moms, major imaging vendors are beginning to use AI to automate the ultrasound process, allowing for lesser trained technicians to provide high quality tests while expanding access to a broader population of women.

AI is being embedded in diagnostic images to mitigate the impact of qualified clinical staff by taking over some of the diagnostic duties typically allocated to humans. For example, AI imaging tools can screen chest X-rays for signs of tuberculosis, often achieving a level of accuracy comparable to humans. This capability could be deployed through an app available to providers in low-resource areas, reducing the need for a trained diagnostic radiologist on-site.[17]

From enabling community-health workers to preventing deadly disease outbreaks before they occur, there is a growing recognition of the tremendous potential of cloud-based AI to eliminate historical obstacles, including daunting shortages of workers, medical equipment, and other resources that require strategic and innovative approaches to overcome. AI tools have an exciting potential not only to optimize existing resources and help overcome these workforce resource shortages but also to greatly improve healthcare delivery and outcomes in low-income settings in ways never previously imagined.

In a collaboration between the Rockefeller Foundation, United States Agency for International Development's (USAID) and the Bill & Melinda Gates Foundation, the groundbreaking report, "AI in Global Health: Defining a Collective Path Forward" was created to explore the current state of the art of AI in healthcare and define use cases with the highest potential improving global health.[18] The use cases defined fall into four categories:

AI-Enabled Population Health: Tools for ingesting, analyzing, and providing recommendations on population health data. This grouping involves tools that leverage AI to monitor and assess population health and select and target public health interventions based on AI-enabled predictive analytics. It includes AI-driven data processing methods that map the spread and burden of disease while AI predictive analytics are then used to project future disease.

Patient Virtual Health Assistant: Tools helping patients direct their own care and wellness, including data-driven diagnostics and recommendations. The use cases in this opportunity area put AI in patients' hands for self-referral, behavioral change, data-driven self-diagnosis, personalized outreach, medical record collection, and AI-facilitated self-care functions. Through the collection of real-time data at the patient level, these AI-enabled tools can help identify the type and severity of a patient's condition and provide health recommendations directly to the patient. Recommendations may include how and where to seek care if it is needed, or guidelines for self-care and behavioral changes to address health issues outside of the health system.

Frontline Health Worker (FHW): Tools augmenting FHW expertise to direct patient care, such as triage and symptom-based diagnostics and care recommendations. This grouping of use cases involves placing AI in the hands of FHWs, enabling them to better serve – and bring top-notch medical technology and advice to – their patients. FHWs in LMICs use AI-enabled tools to triage and diagnose patients (often outside of health facilities) to assist with clinical decision support and to monitor compliance of their patients. Rapid and accurate triage and diagnosis functions are enabled when AI is applied to real-time patient data collected by FHWs. FHWs are then able to provide targeted health recommendations for patients on whether, where, and how to seek care.

Physician Clinical Decision Support: A tool providing specialized expertise to physicians, for example, by enabling a clinician to read diagnostic images. This grouping includes AI use cases that support and improve the decisions of clinical physicians. Examples of AI tools in this grouping are image-based diagnosis support for radiologists and pathologists, decision support tools for clinicians, and quality assurance and training to provide insights for clinicians on past performance, and indicate where errors may have been made (Figure 16.2).

AI-enabled population health	Patient virtual health assistant	FHW virtual health assistant	Physician clinical decision support
Platform ingesting, analyzing, and providing recommendations on population health data	Assisting patients to direct their own care and wellness, e.g, data-driven diagnostics with care recommendations	Augmenting FHW expertise to direct patient care, e.g., triage and symptom-based diagnostics and care recommendations	Providing more specialized expertise to generalist physicians, e.g., enabling a GP to read diagnostic images
• Surveillance and prediction • Population risk management • Intervention selection • Intervention targeting	• Self-referral • Personalized outreach • Behavior change • Data-driven diagnosis • AI-facilitated care • Medical records	• Self-referral • Personalized outreach • Behavior change • Data-driven diagnosis • AI-facilitated care • Medical records	• Image-based diagnosis • Clinical decision support • Quality assurance and training

Figure 16.2   AI groupings for global health use cases. (USAid, Rockefeller Foundation, Bill & Melinda Gates Foundation.)

USING AI TO HELP MANAGE ONE OF THE WORLD'S OLDEST DISEASES

Leprosy is one of the oldest diseases known to humankind, but today an estimated 2 to 3 million people are still living with physical disability and stigmatization of the disease. It often occurs in hard-to-reach communities with poor access to healthcare, where untreated patients continue to spread the infection. Over 200,000 people are newly diagnosed each year – including thousands of children. The lack of progress in eradicating leprosy is partly the result of dwindling attention from health services, decreases in funding, and the absence of new tools to fight the disease.

It is against this backdrop that a new collaboration has come together to leverage the power of the cloud and AI. The Novartis Foundation is a Swiss-based philanthropic organization with a mission of tackling global health challenges and a focus on having a sustainable impact on the health of low-income communities.[19]

The Novartis Foundation is leading a collaboration with the Oswaldo Cruz Foundation (Fiocruz) in Brazil and Microsoft to develop a protocol to examine anonymized images collected by Fiocruz. This will include a high-resolution image and metadata capture protocol to process leprosy skin lesion images. The imagery and AI code will be made publicly available in the form of a leprosy image atlas. The goal is to empower leprosy researchers to accelerate research, accelerate early detection, and prompt treatment, leading to better outcomes in the diagnosis and treatment of this disease.[20]

AI in Health Will Amplify Society

Beyond health, artificial intelligence holds the promise for tremendous societal and economic benefits. The efforts of health leaders to pioneer Intelligent Health Systems is part of a much larger revolution in science, education, government social services, and business. Collectively this will forever change the way we live, work, learn, discover, and communicate.

As most citizens look ahead, they see AI mainly as a force for good. Sixty-three percent agree that AI will help solve complex problems that plague our society and 59% believe it will help people live more fulfilling lives. Only 46% believe AI will harm people by taking away jobs and 23% believe it will have serious, negative implications.[21] As noted in the chart below, there are many societal issues where consumers believe that AI will make a positive contribution to making the world a better place (Figure 16.3).

At a global level, we are already seeing the start of an "AI space race" as countries compete through the development and use of national AI strategies. The United States started the national AI volley in 2016 with the release of its National AI and Research Development Strategic Plan with the goal of guiding investments to produce new AI knowledge and technologies that provide a range of positive benefits to society, while creating a competitive advantage in the global markets. In 2017, China released its country plan declaring AI as a strategic national priority and showcasing the nation's vision for a new national and global economic model driven by AI (Figure 16.4).

As this book went to print there were over 24 countries, including the UK, Japan, and Canada, that had AI country plans completed or under development. In the future AI will create winners and losers in shaping global economies.[22]

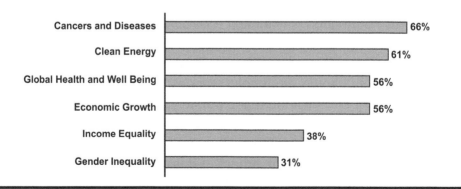

Figure 16.3 **Consumers believe AI will provide solutions to major issues they are concerned with today including the figure. (PWC, Amplifying Humans, 2.0.)**

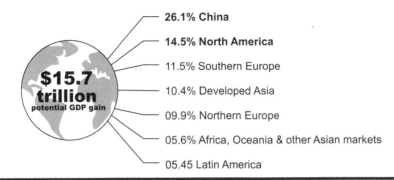

26.1% China

14.5% North America

11.5% Southern Europe

10.4% Developed Asia

09.9% Northern Europe

05.6% Africa, Oceania & other Asian markets

05.45 Latin America

Figure 16.4   The biggest AI gains of China and North America by 2030. (PwC Global Artificial Intelligence Study, 2017.)

AI is the new technology revolution that has the potential to create a world where human abilities are amplified. The question for all to consider is how we will harness this power and the transformational effect it will have on assisting humans in making the planet a better place for all. In this regard, the real story of AI is just a beginning.

Notes

1 Artificial Intelligence and Life in 2030, Stanford University, 2016, https://ai100.stanford.edu/sites/g/files/sbiybj9861/f/ai100report10032016fnl_singles.pdf.
2 Matt Collier, Artificial Intelligence-Healthcare's New Nervous System, Accenture, 2017, www.accenture.com/_acnmedia/pdf-49/accenture-health-artificial-intelligence.pdf#zoom=50.
3 What is Precision Medicine? National Institute of Health, 2018, https://ghr.nlm.nih.gov/primer/precisionmedicine/definition.
4 How We'll Invent the Future, by Bill Gates, *MIT Technology Review*, 2019, www.technologyreview.com/lists/technologies/2019/.
5 Kasey Panetta, The CIO's Guide to Quantum Computing, Gartner, 2019, www.gartner.com/smarterwithgartner/the-cios-guide-to-quantum-computing/.
6 Ibid.
7 Bill Gates, How we'll Invent the Future, by Bill Gates, *MIT Technology Review*, 2019, www.technologyreview.com/lists/technologies/2019/.
8 Ibid.
9 FDA Approves Use of Medtronic Artificial Pancreas, FierceBiotech, 2016, www.fiercebiotech.com/medical-devices/fda-approves-medtronic-s-artificial-pancreas-world-s-first.
10 Laura Donnelly, British Woman Given World's First In-Heart 'Microcomputer', The Telegraph, 2019, www.telegraph.co.uk/news/2019/08/31/british-woman-given-worlds-first-in-heart-microcomputer/amp/.

11 John Paparrizos, MSc, Ryen W. White, PhD, Eric Horvitz, MD, PhD, Screening for pancreatic adenocarcinoma using signals from web search logs: Feasibility study and results, *Journal of Oncology Practice*, 2016, https://ascopubs.org/doi/full/10.1200/JOP.2015.010504.

12 Ibid.

13 Jerry J. Shih, Dean J. Krusienski, Jonathan R. Wolpaw, Brain-computer interfaces in medicine, *Mayo Clinic Proceedings*, 2012, www.ncbi.nlm.nih.gov/pmc/articles/PMC3497935/.

14 Daniela Hernandez, Heather Mack, Elon musk's neuralink shows off advances to brain-computer interface, *The Wall Street Journal*, 2019, www.wsj.com/articles/elon-musks-neuralink-advances-brain-computer-interface-11563334987.

15 American College of Radiology Launches ACR AI-LAB™ to Engage Radiologists in AI Model Development, American College of Radiology, 2019, www.acr.org/Media-Center/ACR-News-Releases/2019/American-College-of-Radiology-Launches-ACR-AILAB-to-Engage-Radiologists-in-AI-Model-Development.

16 Laura Donnelly, Ask Alexa to Diagnose Your Health Problems as NHS Announces 'World-First' Amazon Partnership, The Daily Telegraph, 2019, www.telegraph.co.uk/news/2019/07/09/ask-alexa-diagnose-health-problems-nhs-announces-world-first/?WT.mc_id=tmg_share_tw.

17 Ibid.

18 Artificial Intelligence in Global Health: Defining a Collective Path Forward, USAID, 2019, www.usaid.gov/cii/ai-in-global-health.

19 Novartis Foundation and Microsoft Partner to Develop AI-Enabled Digital Health Tool for Early Leprosy Detection, Novartis Foundation, 2019, www.novartisfoundation.org/news/novartis-foundation-and-microsoft-partner-develop-ai-enabled-digital-health-tool-early-leprosy.

20 Ibid.

21 Bot.Me: A Revolutionary Partnership, PwC, 2017, http://pwcartificialintelligence.com/.

22 Nations Will Spar Over AI, PWC, 2018, www.pwc.com/us/en/services/consulting/library/artificial-intelligence-predictions/ai-arms-race.html.

Index